Turn everyday items like rice, food coloring, tissue paper,
glue, yogurt containers and dishwashing liquid
into hours of creative fun for your toddler or preschool child.

GREAT EXPLORATIONS helps you make the most of your child's growing curiosity through activities that encourage experimentation and exploration. Each chapter offers clear instructions for how to engage your child in a variety of stimulating, self-directed projects. You can introduce your child to the world of:

▶ Wearable art—from homemade hats to tissue paper necklaces

▶ Science—building a bird feeder, fishing with magnets, and much more

▶ Seasonal activities—from making special-occasion cards to printing with fall leaves

▶ Cooking—no-bake cookies, homemade butter, and other easy-to-make treats

▶ Things to do outside—snow pictures, obstacle course

▶ Music and movement activities, pretend play ideas, and many other delightful things to do. . . .

GREAT EXPLORATIONS

100 Creative Play Ideas for Parents and Preschoolers from Playspace at

The
Children's
Museum
Boston

Written by Amy Nolan
Illustrated by Kim Gulino

POCKET BOOKS
New York   London   Toronto   Sydney   Tokyo   Singapore

An *Original* Publication of POCKET BOOKS

POCKET BOOKS, a division of Simon & Schuster Inc.
1230 Avenue of the Americas, New York, NY 10020

The Children's Museum Boston   Copyright © 1997 by The Boston Children's Museum

Library of Congress Cataloging-in-Publication Data

Nolan, Amy.
    Great explorations : 100 creative play ideas for parents and preschoolers from Playspace at the Children's Museum, Boston / written by Amy Nolan ; illustrated by Kim Gulino.
        p.   cm.
    ISBN: 0-671-52857-2
    1. Creative activities and seat work.   2. Education, Preschool— Activity programs.   3. Education, Preschool—Parent participation. I. Children's Museum of Boston.   II. Title.
    LB1140.35.C74N65   1997
    372.21—dc21   97-27502
                                                    CIP

First Pocket Books trade paperback printing December 1997

10 9 8 7 6 5 4 3 2

POCKET and colophon are registered trademarks of Simon & Schuster Inc.

Cover design by Jeanne M. Lee
Text design by Stanley S. Drate/Folio Graphics Co. Inc.

Printed in the U.S.A.

For Barbara,
Thank you for bringing joy and music into all of our lives.

ACKNOWLEDGMENTS

I would like to thank the staff members of the Museum's Early Childhood Program for their support and dedication to this project. Thanks to:

Jeri Robinson for her leadership and for her promise to me that this book would be written someday.

Barbara Goldfinger for contributing her Music and Movement activities. Also for her comments and careful editing which kept me on track throughout the writing process.

Natalie Zigmont for her many contributions to the activities and her flexibility in accommodating all of my questions and special requests.

Kacy Hughes for acting as my liaison and helping me sort through the red tape.

Claudia Fonseca for her "Going Fishing" activity and her useful suggestions.

Special thanks to Leslie Swartz, Director of Education, for her role in the publishing process.

Thanks to our terrific and easygoing editor, Leslie Stern.

CONTENTS

1 Playspace Favorites—Arts and Crafts   *15*

2 Science Is Fun

3 Things to Do Outside

4 Seasonal Activities

FALL

WINTER

SPRING

5 Quiet Activities

6 Music and Movement

7 Pretend Play

8 Cooking

9 "How To" for Parents

FOREWORD

Play is the way the child learns what no one can teach him.

L. K. FRANK

For almost fifteen years, parents and preschoolers have been visiting Playspace at The Children's Museum. Playspace offers children under the age of five a place to do the serious work of childhood: playing and growing. Playspace is an area of the museum designed specifically for preschoolers, toddlers, and their parents and care-givers.

The Children's Museum created Playspace in 1978 in response to a growing trend. Although most of the Museum's exhibits were geared for older children, we were seeing an increase in the number of preschoolers visiting. Now, close to half of our visitors are parents and children under the age of five and Playspace is a favorite spot for many of them.

Our visitors range from families on vacation to "regulars" who come with their children on a weekly basis to play and take part in our programs. Our activities need to be successful and interesting for all parents and children under five, both onetime and weekly visitors.

Children are the exhibit in Playspace. Here, infants, toddlers, preschoolers, and children with special needs can find toys and activities helpful to their learning and growth. Playspace is designed like a large indoor playground, one in which children may move freely from one activity to another while parents may choose to join in or watch their child play. Just as children grow, parents are also learning and growing.

Parents learn through talking with each other or by watching other parents. The seating areas are made up of large semicircular benches that encourage conversation and comfort.

You will find children playing at their own pace and level of development in Playspace. Infants can explore the tunnel, soft play nest, and an assortment of stacking, rolling, and musical toys in the infant area. Older toddlers and preschoolers can keep busy cooking and cleaning in the kitchen and dress-up corner. Children in a more active mood can use their imaginations and their muscles on our multilevel castle and slide. Our other two corners feature an old-fashioned car and gas pump and a large train set. Nooks and crannies give kids a place to build with blocks, play with letters, draw with chalk, play some bells, or read a book.

In the center of Playspace is our activity table, which gives children the opportunity to explore different mediums and materials. You may find children playing with play dough, paint, or paste along with their parents and one of our staff.

Our activities provide a variety of learning experiences that we see as a foundation for many of the skills a child needs in order to be successful in school and at home. Children can practice their motor skills while learning how to use a paintbrush; they practice their sharing skills by playing with other children at the sand table. With these activities, children learn about many things, including color mixing; the textures of sand and paint; how to make a line; and how to pour and measure. Children also begin to understand the concepts of "shape" and "line" and "empty" and "full."

Our activities operate on a drop-in basis. Children may join or leave an activity according to their interest and ability. The allure of the project table is natural curiosity. Children and parents see other children busy with play dough and want to do it too.

Generally, the children need very little introduction to materials. They operate with their own built-in agenda and are adept at using whatever is set before them, although not necessarily in the way in which adults intend it to be used. A child may enjoy painting with paste and a brush, yet may not be interested when you add colored tissue to make a collage.

For you, the lesson to be learned from the activity may be as simple as taking a moment to sit back and watch your child. Each child has a unique style all her own that merits appreciation. We encourage you to be flexible about the outcome of activities and your definition of success. It is important to remember that your child's choice of approach is due in part to her level of development.

Visiting parents often ask us questions that start with, "I have an eighteen-month-old," or "I have a two-and-a-half-year-old; do you have any ideas about things I can do with her at home?" We started writing down some of our most popular activities, like our play dough recipe, for people to take home with them. Visitors were pleased to get our handouts and continued to ask for more information about our projects. They are a way for people to take something educational home with them from their museum experience. We have since put all of our curriculum into writing, and have created *Great Explorations*.

Great Explorations focuses on art, science, music, cooking, and dramatic play experiences that encompass a discovery-based approach to learning. With this approach, there is no right or wrong and you learn as you go along. All of our activities are age appropriate, varied, open ended, creative, and fun, yet also simple and inexpensive to re-create in other settings. Our goal is for our activities and materials to be as accessible as possible to as many people as possible.

We chose activities that have been Playspace favorites with children, parents, and staff over the years, as well as popular new activities. *Great Explorations* is intended to serve as a helping hand both for parents in need of an introduction to "playing" with their children and for experienced professionals who are looking for new ideas.

GREAT EXPLORATIONS

INTRODUCTION

What is our philosophy?

Our philosophy in Playspace centers around the idea that play is one of the most important ways in which children learn and grow. One of the best ways to get to know your child is through play. Parents can learn about their children's likes and dislikes, their talents, their hopes and fears and their dreams.

We believe that understanding your child's motivations enables you to be a more capable and effective parent. We see parenting as a complex and sometimes overwhelming responsibility. Our goal is to support parents with young children by providing them with useful educational resources.

Why are play and exploration important? What can these experiences do for my child's development and self-esteem?

We believe that "play is a child's work" and that play and exploration are the vehicles through which children learn. Play is an essential part of a child's development that should be encouraged. Parents can provide children with rich settings in which to play and explore.

Children are born eager to learn. Whether a baby is learning to sit up on his own or a toddler is learning to paint a picture, children learn by doing. By exposing your child to science, art, music, and more, you can give your child's education a head start.

The activities in this book were designed for toddlers and preschoolers to provide well-rounded experiences for their personal development. A wide variety of learning experiences like these can translate into building confidence, skills, and abilities that will stay with children all of their lives.

What is my role as a parent?

As a parent, you play an invaluable role as your child's first teacher. Parents provide their children with the foundation skills they will need as they grow. Spending quality time on educational activities introduces your child to new ideas and nourishes the bond between you and your child. Participating actively in your child's learning is a step toward ensuring your child's success at school and at home.

What guidelines should I keep in mind when I try these activities?

Essentially, the important thing to remember is that these activities are not about the "right" or "wrong" way to paint or paste. You don't have to "instruct" your child about the proper way to use the materials. Whenever possible, present the materials with a short explanation and then allow your child to control the direction that the activity takes. Often children can learn more and have a more meaningful experience when they figure things out on their own, at their own pace. Your child may not yet be able to complete the activity in a single session, but the time spent may be more meaningful to her because she has made the important connections for herself.

As you participate in the activities described in this book, you may find that becoming sensitive to your child's learning needs takes some practice. If you are unsure about when to step back and when to offer assistance, take a moment to read the boxes and additional sections that accompany the activities. You will find many useful tips about how the projects work and ways that you can be involved.

Always keep in mind that these projects are supposed to be fun. Pace the activity according to your child's interest or age level. Even if you spend only five minutes playing with rice, it is still worthwhile as a learning experience, provided you don't mind cleaning up. Every little bit of exposure is valuable, even if at the time it seems too short to be significant. As your child grows, these experiences will be linked together to form a broader understanding.

How do children learn and grow with these activities?

Each time a child comes to these activities, she is able to use the materials in a new way. It is a question of building skills slowly over time. For example, a young child who is given a crayon to hold on to will eventually manage to make her first mark, a single scratched line. As she practices with the crayon and she continues to grow, she will develop coordination and motor skills. With time, she is able to draw a circle. Later, with more practice, growth, and focus, she can make a drawing of everyone in her family, complete with arms, legs, fingers, and toes.

In this way, as your child continues to change and grow on a daily basis, the information and skills that he brings to an activity will influence the outcome. Whether you are building with blocks, pouring water from one container to another, or dancing to music, each time you try an activity there will be a different result. Each experience reflects where she is at that moment in her development. We encourage you to repeat each activity many times because children master skills through repetition.

Why did we pick these activities? What do we hope that you will get out of them?

We wanted to show parents that without spending much money, we have in our homes many of the materials we need to set up exciting and creative activities for our children. The activities and materials we chose are varied and interesting, covering a range of concepts and skills.

We specifically chose activities that are creative and non-competitive in nature. In this way, regardless of your child's developmental level, she will have a successful experience, simply by being involved. Our approach is "process oriented," meaning that although most of the art activities end in a finished product, the painting your child made is not the most important part. We feel that the real learning is in the experimentation that took your child from the starting point to the finished picture.

We hope that this book will serve as a springboard for your own explorations, opening up creative avenues and resources so that you can personalize favorite activities or come up with new ones. It is our wish that these activities will inspire many creative play ideas in your home.

Why did we choose these subjects for our chapters?

Playspace Favorites—Arts and Crafts

Art is a form of communication; it is a way of expressing feelings and exploring the possibilities that arise when you combine imagination and materials. Art is immediate. Making a bold, sweeping line gives your child the feeling of satisfaction. Like photographs, art projects preserve a snippet in time, serving as a benchmark for your child's growth and development.

Science Is Fun

Early science activities like measuring, pouring, and mixing colors build a foundation for the understanding of basic math and other more abstract concepts. For example, when learning to count, children need to learn that the number 1 stands for one unit, like a cup of rice. "How many cups of rice will it take to fill this container? Let's count. One, two, three." Also, knowing the colors allows children to begin to group similar objects. "How many green circles are there? How many red squares?"

Things to Do Outside

These activities are most appropriate for warm weather outdoors, but all of these activities can be moved inside as well. Each activity page has instructions for using the materials successfully inside your home. Playspace at The Children's Museum has no outside facility. Despite our limitations and the large volume of our visitors, we run many activities that are traditionally thought of as messy. All of our hints and tips for minimizing mess have been included in this chapter.

Seasonal Activities

Seasonal activities give children a feel for the rhythm and cycle of the seasons. This chapter combines art, music, dance, and more to highlight each season and its corresponding holidays. A seasonal song or activity can turn a regular day into a special one. Sing a song, take a walk, and talk to your child about what is unique about this particular time of the year.

Quiet Activities

The designation of "quiet" simply means that you can use these activities to help your child to wind down. These activities are intended to be appropriate for quiet time at home, both indoors and out.

Music and Movement

Music and movement activities give children confidence and teach them to take pride in their own uniqueness and creativity. Songs emphasize the lyrical qualities of language and help your child learn to listen carefully. Movement activities are a powerful way for a child to express herself by getting in touch with her body and feelings. Both songs and movement activities are also a positive way for her to release tension and excess energy.

Pretend Play

Not only is pretend play an important component of a healthy childhood, it's also a lot of fun. Making up stories and acting out scenarios is one way in which children prepare to be "grown up." Our activities will provide the backdrop so that you can tap into your child's imagination. Let the role-play begin!

Cooking

Cooking is really science. When you cook you are combining different ingredients and noticing changes that occur. Aside from its more scientific aspects, cooking can also be the perfect opportunity for little "helpers." Since mealtime is often family time, including your child in mealtime preparation allows her to make a contribution to the family. She is also learning to make healthy choices about the foods she eats.

"How To" for Parents

With all of the toys available today, it is still nice to know that you can take everyday materials and make a simple toy for your child that has "play appeal." There is a feeling of satisfaction that comes from making something for your child by hand. These projects demonstrate the value of ingenuity and doing things for yourself.

What makes this book different from other activity books for kids?

This book is unique for a number of reasons. Most important, this book was designed especially for parents. Many books for preschoolers are written for professional educators. We were interested in creating a parent-friendly publication that would be easy to read and understand, even with a young child tugging at your sleeve. We wanted to make the activities clear and the supplies basic and inexpensive, so that parents could try these projects at home.

The activities we included represent a comprehensive learning program for preschoolers, with a focus on developing the "whole" child. Our program includes art, science, dramatic play, toys and games, music, and cooking. Many books cover only one of these subject areas. Within each chapter of our book, you will find learning experiences with ties to areas like language development, reading, math, science, problem solving, and self-expression. Because it was intended for parents, each activity is accompanied by a section called "What Your Child Is Learning," which highlights the educational concepts involved.

Our fundamental approach centers around discovery. We feel that a child's early learning should not be "product" oriented. As a result, our activities are structured so that there is no right or wrong way to approach them. We believe that often when meaningful learning occurs, the end result may not be a finished object. Although children need materials to handle in order to learn, in the end learning is an internal process.

One benefit of our open-ended approach is that young toddlers who are often thought of as being "too young" can participate in these activities. Many activity books tend to concentrate on projects for three- to five-year-olds. However, we've found that there are a multitude of age-appropriate activities for younger children and we wanted to share these activities with you. The majority of our activities are suited for children between eighteen months and five years old. You will even find activities for children as young as one year old. These activities have been tested by hundreds of young toddlers and are perfect introductions to new materials, ideas, and processes.

Where do I start?

The activities in this book complement one another, but are not meant to be done in any particular order. You choose where you want to begin. If you like, you can browse through the book and see what catches your eye. Simply use our guidelines to match your child's age with an activity that looks interesting to you. If you are looking for a seasonal project or an activity for a special occasion, check the Contents. We've grouped our projects into categories like "Things to Do Outside," "Arts and Crafts," and "Quiet Activities" so that it's easy to find the right activity.

Because time is often a factor, we have included a time key to give you an idea of how much time you will need for each project. The time we assigned to each project refers to the approximate time that most children will spend with the materials themselves. The time indicated does not reflect setup or cleanup time. Plan to give yourself about fifteen extra minutes to allow for setup and cleanup of most projects.

Before you begin, read the section under "Getting Started" (pp. 9–10). This information covers what supplies you will need and how to set up activities in your home. You may choose to buy general supplies that you can use for many activities or just pick up a few things at first, like the materials for play dough. Use this book as you would use a cookbook; combine activities to plan an interesting "menu," and add some original materials or variations, as you would personalize spices in a recipe.

If you are planning to do a project, particularly an art project, you may want to try the project yourself the night before you introduce it to your child. This will give you a chance to see how the activity works and think through how your child will use the materials. This way, you can anticipate what to expect when you try it together. This is especially helpful with older children, ages three and up, who often appreciate having an example of the finished project to look at to give them ideas for their own creations.

Now you are ready for your first activity. Start with an activity that you feel comfortable with. Relax and have fun. Use the fifteen- or twenty-minute time frame to focus only on your child. Think of yourself not as a teacher but as an observer and helper.

Enjoy your special time together. We wish you the best of luck!

GETTING STARTED

What do I really need?

You will find that a few versatile supplies can be used for many of our activities. Other supplies and specialty items can be added later on. If you would like to buy a stock of supplies so that you will have the materials called for in most of our activities, we recommend that you start with the following items:

a plastic painter's tarp or shower curtain to protect your floor
a plastic place mat for your child to work on
a smock or old adult-sized shirt for your child to wear
construction paper in assorted colors, at least 8½ by 11 inches
tissue paper in assorted colors
a set of watercolor markers
a package of jumbo crayons
tempera paint (one color to start)
a child's paintbrush or a foam-tipped brush from the hardware store
food coloring
flour
salt
rice
cookie cutters
a dishwashing tub
plastic cups, bowls, spoons

yarn
a box of pasta (ziti or rigatoni)
a hole punch
scissors (adult)
cellophane tape
masking tape
paste or glue and a brush (see "How to Make a Paste and Paint Brush," p. 210)
Joy dishwashing liquid
sponges
Styrofoam supermarket trays (two or three)
yogurt containers with lids (one or two)
old clothing and accessories for dress-up

Note: For more information on where to buy supplies or for a more comprehensive list of materials see the Appendix "Where to Buy Supplies" p. 239.

How can I store the supplies?

Plastic storage bins with lids are a perfect place to store supplies. They are inexpensive, come in many sizes, and can be purchased from discount supply stores. In Playspace, we stack our bins and store them on shelves. For easy access, use a label sticker and a permanent marker to label a side panel with a list of what's inside. Or choose a bin with a clear plastic bottom so that you can see the contents.

ABOUT SETTING UP ACTIVITIES

Where should I set up the activities?

Create an area for your child where it is okay to experiment with the materials without worrying about the floor, furniture, or other items nearby. When the weather permits, do messy projects outside. Inside, create a space where your child can explore, preferably on a table over tile, linoleum, or bare floor rather than carpeting.

What can I do to keep things clean?

The single biggest thing that you can do to keep things neat is to supervise your child closely. It only takes a minute for a bucket to be overturned or a jar of paint to be knocked over.

Before using projects involving materials like paint, glue, water, food coloring, rice, or sand, line the floor and the work surface with a protective cloth. Drop cloths made from plastic, vinyl, or heavy fabric are preferred because they will contain spills. For additional cleaning needs, always keep a damp sponge nearby.

Another helpful hint: put out only as much of a messy material as your child will need. Always keep any full jars of paint, food coloring, or other spillables out of your child's reach. Take the time to put extra supplies away before you start the activity. In the event of a spill, a small quantity of paint in a container is easier to handle than a full jar.

Can I use newspaper to cover the floor?

Newspaper is fine for covering the work surface, and in a pinch you can use it on the floor. But it tends to get kicked around and bunched up under your child's feet, which ultimately leads to more mess. We suggest that you use a shower curtain or a plastic painter's tarp from the hardware store. The painter's tarp should be at least 2 mil. thick.

How should I present the art materials?

The golden rule is less is more. Set out the materials a little at a time so that your child can see all of them. Too much to choose from can make things confusing for young children. Place items within your child's reach. Remember to use a plastic place mat or other washable surface for your child to work on. Loose items like paper scraps can be placed in a shoe box or small plastic basket. When using materials that may spill, like water or paint, dole out the materials in very small portions to minimize mess.

In Playspace we have had to master how to use potentially messy materials like paint and glue. We work with large groups of children and no running water. We have included all of our suggestions for how to use these types of materials while maintaining your low blood pressure. If you take a few minutes to read the suggestion boxes in each chapter, it may make you feel more comfortable trying the activities.

Can I use rice, sand, or water inside?

Yes. The key to using materials like water, sand, or rice successfully lies in making sure that the materials are contained so that you are able to clean up easily. To accomplish this when you are inside, use only a moderate amount of water or rice, and a plastic or vinyl tarp. The container you use should be large enough to keep most of the materials inside without spilling over. Keep the materials in a container in the center of the tarp, so that you can quickly mop or scoop up any mess. Supervise your child closely. We recommend keeping a mop, Dustbuster or vacuum cleaner nearby.

I turned around for a moment and my child colored on the wall! What should I do if she uses the art materials in the wrong place?

It is common for young children to use materials inappropriately, because they are learning the rules as they go along. If your child goes from drawing on her paper to drawing on the table or wall next to her, try to react calmly. Often it will suffice to tell her that drawing is done on paper. You can then redirect her gently to an appropriate use for the materials.

How do I remove marks or stains on the table or wall?

To remove any stray crayon marks from walls or tables, use an automotive hand cleaner with lanolin, such as DL hand cleaner, and a clean cloth. Tempera paints can be removed with soap and water. Stubborn paint stains can be removed with hand cleaner or bleach. Bleach is recommended to remove stains from man-made surfaces like counters, tabletops, chairs, or place mats. The ratio that we use is one part bleach to ten parts water. This solution cleans and disinfects toys and work surfaces. However, bleach is not recommended for woodwork or painted surfaces.

What about stains on clothes?

Pretreat clothes that are soiled with a spray-on or rub-on stain-removing solution. Although most children's materials are intended to be washable, unfortunately, some are more washable than others. When purchasing supplies, look for the words *washable* or *water soluble* on the label. However, the best way to avoid ruining your child's best outfit is to dress her in old clothes for projects.

CHAPTER 1
Playspace Favorites

Arts and Crafts

Homemade Hats

▶ **AGES:**
18 months to 4+ years

▶ **ACTIVITY TIME:**
10 to 20 minutes

Materials

- ◆ a long strip of heavy paper or light-weight cardboard long enough to wrap around your child's head and wide enough (about 3 to 6 inches) to decorate
- ◆ scrap materials like magazine cuttings, paper pieces, shiny paper, colored tissue, yarn, or cotton balls
- ◆ paste or glue and a brush*
- ◆ masking tape or a stapler
- ◆ newspaper, place mat, or plastic tray to paste on
- ◆ a wet cloth for washing fingers

Activity

Place the scrap materials, the paste or glue, and the paper strip on the work surface. Encourage your child to explore the paste or glue with some of the different materials. Give him time to make his own choices about how he would like to decorate his hat.

Watch what your child does with the materials. There is no right or wrong way to use them. Whatever your child does, no matter what it ends up looking like, he is still learning.

When he is done, staple or tape the ends of the paper together so that it fits around his head. Make sure that the edges of the staples are on the outside of the hat facing away from your child. For dirty fingers, use a wet cloth.

*To make your own brush, see "How to Make a Paste and Paint Brush," p. 210.

What Your Child Is Learning

A child's creation is special. When he has the opportunity to wear and show his creation, it brings pride and a sense of accomplishment. Hats have special significance because of their role-playing capabilities. Putting on a hat can free a child's imagination to be anything he wants to be.

More Things to Do

Make a bracelet and necklace to match the hat! See instructions for "Tissue Paper Bracelets" and "Tissue Paper Necklaces," which follow.

Make a crown! Cut triangles into the top edge of a piece of paper big enough to fit your child's head. Wrap the paper with aluminum foil. Have your child decorate it with paste and bits of paper. Fold and staple it to fit your child's head.

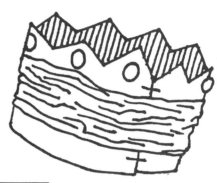

▶ Talk to your child about what things feel and look like. "Cotton balls are soft and round. The silver paper is shiny and smooth." Art and science projects are wonderful opportunities to increase your child's vocabulary.

▶ Wallpaper is not just for walls! Many stores that carry wallpaper will give away books of discontinued patterns. These books are terrific for collage projects.

Tissue Paper Bracelets

▶ **AGES:**
18 months to 4+ years

▶ **ACTIVITY TIME:**
10 to 20 minutes

Materials
- a strip of heavy paper or lightweight cardboard 6 to 8 inches in length
- tissue or shiny paper cut into squares and long strips
- paste or glue and a brush*
- masking tape or a stapler
- newspaper, place mat, or plastic tray to paste on
- a wet cloth for washing fingers

Activity

Put out the tissue strips, heavy paper or cardboard strip, and paste. Let your child experiment with gluing or pasting the pieces of tissue paper onto the heavy paper strip.

Make streamers by pasting long, thin pieces of tissue onto the strip. Overlapping pieces of tissue will create new colors. Try making "flowers" by crunching up small pieces of tissue.

When your child is done, staple or tape the ends of the cardboard together so that the bracelet fits around his wrist. Make sure that the edges of the staples are on the outside, facing away from him. A wet cloth can be used to clean up dirty fingers.

*To make your own brush, see "How to Make a Paste and Paint Brush," p. 210.

What Your Child Is Learning

Your child is developing his imagination and esthetic sensibilities with this activity. He is making choices about colors and shapes that are interesting to him with each piece of tissue that he pastes. Color overlaps teach him about the new colors they create. "What happened when you put the yellow piece on top of the blue one?" Children are proud to wear something they have created.

More Things to Do

Make a hat! Let the child decorate an 18- by 24-inch piece of paper with tissue. Roll the paper into a cone shape to fit the child's head. Staple or tape the edges.

Design a necklace! See instructions for "Tissue Paper Necklaces" (p. 22).

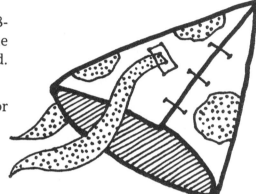

Paper Belts

► AGES:
18 months to 4+ years

► ACTIVITY TIME:
5 to 20 minutes

Materials

- a long, thin strip of tagboard or lightweight cardboard long enough to wrap around your child's waist, overlapping about 3 inches. The paper should be wide enough (about 3 to 6 inches) to decorate
- collage materials like wrapping paper, magazine cuttings, paper pieces, shiny paper, colored tissue, yarn, or cotton balls
- paste or glue and a paste brush*
- scissors or a hole punch
- a pencil
- a piece of yarn or string 8 to 10 inches long
- newspaper, place mat, or plastic tray to paste on
- a wet washcloth for clean up

Activity

Arrange the paper, paste, and collage materials on the table. Show your child how paste helps things to stick. Then let her explore some of the different materials on her own. For dirty fingers, use a wet cloth.

When she is finished, allow the paper to dry thoroughly. When it's dry, bend the paper into a loop, overlapping about 3 inches. Mark a spot with a pencil, about 2 inches from the end of the top piece, in the center. This is going to be the "buckle."

With scissors or a hole punch, make a hole at the mark that goes through both layers of paper.

*To make your own brush, see "How to Make Your Own Paste and Paint Brush," p. 210.

Thread the yarn through the hole. Bring the other end of the yarn around and tie the ends together to make a bow. Your child can now take her belt on and off.

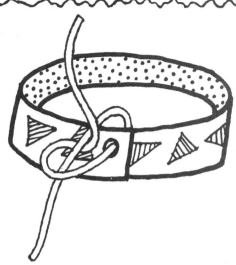

What Your Child Is Learning

Making her own belt is a way for your child to gain experience using art materials creatively. It is exciting for children to make something that they can use. Making and wearing a homemade belt encourages imagination. She can use the homemade belt as the beginning of a dress-up wardrobe to turn today into a special occasion.

More Things to Do

For children under three: See instructions for other collage projects.

Ages three and up: Create a whole outfit! Your belt could be the centerpiece of an original ensemble.

Paint a white T-shirt with fabric paint! (Remember to stuff the T-shirt with newspaper so that the painting doesn't go through the material to the back of the shirt.)

Note: When buying crafts supplies like fabric paint that is not designed specifically for children, always look for the word *nontoxic* on the label before purchasing.

▶ *Parent quote: "Sarah loves to collage, but she is more interested in the paste than in the things to stick on. She can sit there for hours and be perfectly happy, with just the paste and the brush."*

It's natural for children to be more interested in exploring than in making a picture. They are still learning about the paste and what it feels like to use. After a few experiences with paste, they will be ready to try the collage materials.

Tissue Paper Necklaces

► AGES:
18 months to 4+ years

► ACTIVITY TIME:
15 to 30 minutes

Note: This project requires ten to fifteen minutes of preparation. To begin you'll need:

♦ cardboard to cut into shapes
♦ heavy-duty scissors or a utility knife to cut cardboard

(1)
CUT OUT
CARDBOARD
SHAPES

Ahead of time, cut the cardboard into small shapes between 2 and 5 inches in length and width. Squares, triangles, circles, and rainbows are good shapes to make. For young toddlers or children trying this activity for the first time, three or four cardboard shapes should be enough to start with.

Materials

♦ multicolored tissue paper cut into small pieces
♦ a hole punch
♦ paste and a paste brush*
♦ yarn or string 14 to 16 inches long
♦ a piece of tape
♦ a wet cloth for washing fingers
♦ newspaper, place mat, or plastic tray to cover the work surface

(2)
PREPARE
ENDS OF
THREADER

Activity

Wrap a piece of tape around one end of the piece of string so that it comes to a point to help your child thread the yarn through the

*To make your own brush, see "How to Make a Paste and Paint Brush" (p. 210).

cardboard shapes. Tie a double knot with the other end of the string so that the shapes won't slip off the string.

Put out some cardboard pieces, tissue paper, paste, and a brush. Encourage your child to paste the pieces of tissue paper onto the cardboard any way she likes.

Since tissue paper is translucent when it is pasted, your child can make different combinations of colors by layering.

When she is finished with a cardboard shape, punch a hole in the top with a hole punch. Together, string the cardboard shape onto the yarn. You can tie knots on either side of the cardboard shape to keep it in place.

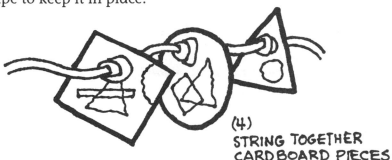

(3)
PASTE ON
TISSUE AND
PUNCH HOLE

(4)
STRING TOGETHER
CARDBOARD PIECES

What Your Child Is Learning

Your child is learning how to recognize and discriminate between different colors and shapes. You can help by talking about shapes: "We just finished pasting a square. I wonder how many sides it has. Let's count them. Next we'll count the sides on the triangle. Boy, that circle sure looks different from the others. How many sides does it have?"

▶ Resist the urge to hurry your child or get her to try something else unless she seems to be stuck. If you think she might need help, ask her before giving her a hand.

More Things to Do

Make a matching hat and bracelet! See instructions for "Homemade Hats" (p. 16) and "Tissue Paper Bracelets"(p. 18).

See what else you can string! Try stringing pastas like rigatoni or ziti to add to your necklace. See "Stringing Beads," which follows, and "How to Dye Pasta" (p. 215).

▶ *What will his project look like?*

Children just want to explore, whereas adults are more interested in the final product. The challenge is to set aside expectations and follow your child's lead.

▶ *Parent quote:* "I think that it's really important for my daughter to work things out for herself. It's hard. Sometimes I have to remind myself that it's her project, not mine."

Stringing Beads

► **AGES:**
12 months to 4+ years

► **ACTIVITY TIME:**
10 to 20 minutes

Materials

Ages one to two
♦ large plastic pop beads

Ages two to three
♦ a thick lace or yarn stiffened at one end with a piece of tape for stringing
♦ an assortment of items to string, such as: large wooden beads or plastic spools at least 2 inches in diameter
uncooked pasta with large holes in the center like ziti or rigatoni
construction paper or cardboard shapes with holes punched in the center

Ages three to four
♦ any of the above plus smaller wooden and plastic beads
♦ buttons, plastic straws cut into pieces, and plastic lacing
♦ washers and nuts from your toolbox or a hardware store

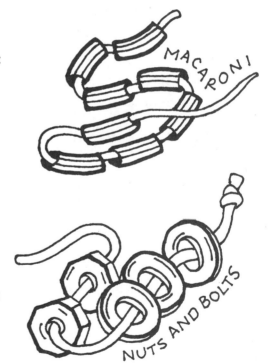

PLASTIC POP BEADS

MACARONI

NUTS AND BOLTS

Activity   **Age one to two:** Using the plastic pop beads, show your child how to pull them apart and then push them together. Put together a long string of beads and let your child pull them apart.

   Age two and three: Put out a variety of things to string of different colors, shapes, and sizes. Show your child how to string items using the lace or yarn taped at one end. She may enjoy taking the necklace apart afterward.

   Age three to four: Your child can begin to string smaller beads onto shoelaces and plastic lacing. She may also enjoy stringing a necklace with colored beads that create a simple pattern of two or three alternating colors, for example: yellow, blue, yellow, blue, etc.

What Your Child Is Learning   Stringing is good for classifying or grouping like and unlike objects. "How many red things can we string?" Or, "Can you find another piece that looks like this one?" For older kids, stringing beads is a great way to begin to develop counting skills. Older children can also invent some simple patterns. Count with your child as you string. It is a chance for her to begin to learn that the numbers one, two, and three stand for real objects.

More Things to Do   Dye pasta with food coloring to make colorful homemade necklaces. See instructions for "How to Dye Pasta," p. 215.

   For children three and up, try stringing Cheerios. It's challenging, and the result is edible!

   For children three and up, make beads out of play dough. See the "Play Dough Recipes" on p. 50. Once the child is done making her beads, poke a hole through the top with a toothpick and allow the beads to dry. The play dough can also be painted with watercolor or tempera paint.

▶ *Does your child need practice learning to hold on to things? Working with beads helps your child develop the small motor skills needed to grasp and manipulate objects.*

Hand Prints

▶ AGES:
12 months to 4+ years

▶ ACTIVITY TIME:
5 to 15 minutes

Materials

- finger paint or liquid tempera paint
- dishwashing liquid
- heavy paper, at least 8½ by 11 inches
- a sponge (4 by 6 inches)
- a spoon
- a dishpan with soapy water and paper towels
- newspaper or plastic place mat to print on

Activity

In Playspace, we mix finger paint or liquid tempera paint with a few drops of dishwashing liquid when we make hand prints. This makes cleanup easier.

Start with a damp sponge. Next, squirt three or four drops of dishwashing liquid into the middle of the sponge. Fold the sponge in half and squeeze it to distribute the soap. Apply a thin coat of paint to the sponge with the back of a spoon or a knife. Scrape off the excess.

Place the paint sponge next to a piece of paper. Have a dishpan of soapy water nearby for speedy cleanup.

Show your child how to press his hand onto the sponge so that there is a light coating of paint on his hand. Have him press his hand on a piece of heavy paper.

What Your Child Is Learning

Hand prints help your child develop body awareness and also serve as a record of your child's growth. Making an imprint of a child's hand also shows the child that he is individual and special, which fosters self-esteem. For older children, this project can reinforce the concept of themselves as independent people with their own wishes and desires. Make your own hand print along with your child.

More Things to Do

Make a picture with lots of hand prints. What happens when you overlap them or use different colors?

Make foot prints! Cover the floor with newspaper. Ask your child to sit in a chair. Place the paint sponge in a dishpan at the foot of the chair, next to a large piece of heavy paper. He can step onto the sponge and then walk across the paper.

Together, look at your child's hand and foot prints from when he was born and talk to him about how he's grown.

Crazy Collages

► AGES:
12 months to 4 years

► ACTIVITY TIME:
5 to 20 minutes

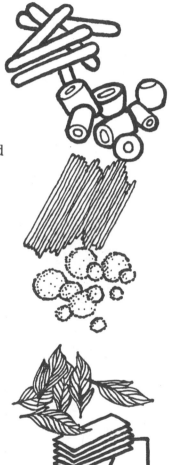

Materials

- scrap materials like magazine cuttings, wrapping paper scraps, paper pieces, shiny paper, yarn, and cotton balls
- paste and a paste brush*
- background paper like construction paper or poster board
- a smock or old adult-sized shirt for your child to wear
- a plastic place mat or newspaper to paste on

Activity

Place the background paper on the table along with a small container of paste, a paste brush, and a variety of collage materials.

Encourage your child to explore the paste and different materials, finding out what sticks and doesn't stick with paste. There is no right or wrong way to use these materials. Whatever your child does or doesn't do, no matter what it ends up looking like, it is all part of learning.

Collage is often a child's favorite project. For variety, try different shapes and types of background paper. Use materials with different textures, even things like pieces of sandpaper, felt scraps, and pieces of torn tissue paper.

*To make your own brush, see "How to Make a Paste and Paint Brush," p. 210.

What Your Child Is Learning

Exploration with the materials develops creativity and self-expression. Each piece that your child adds is a decision about what is important to her. It is this arrangement or juxtaposition of pieces that makes each collage unique. You can emphasize those choices by asking your child about the colors she is using. Talk to her about specific things in her picture that are interesting to you. "I like how you put this small square next to the blue circle. What shape are you going to use next?"

▶ *Staff quote:* "I love watching the kids at the activity table. The little kids take these projects so seriously and they all have very different ways of working. With collage, some kids will pile things on top of each other in the middle of their paper. Others spread their pieces out so that they won't touch each other. The three- and four-year-olds can tell you stories about their pictures and the really young kids sometimes eat the paste!"

More Things to Do

Cut the background paper into the shape of a flower and decorate it with brightly colored tissue.

Make a tissue paper collage! Thin some white glue with a little water, so that it is runny. For best results, choose a light-colored piece of paper for the background. Lay the tissue paper in place on the picture and brush the glue mixture over it. Children can add pieces of tissue and make different color combinations by brushing the glue over the layered tissue. Dry on a flat surface.

Try adding food coloring or powdered tempera paint to paste or glue.

With children ages three and up, try making your own paste with flour and water. Add water gradually to a small cup of flour and stir. It is a little lumpy, but fun to try.

▶ *Parent quote:* "The first time my child used paste, he managed to eat as much as he put on his paper. I wondered whether or not he was too young to be trying this, but I figured it couldn't hurt him. That's what kids his *age* do. That's how they learn about things. Luckily, after tasting it once or twice, he was not too anxious to repeat the experience."

▶ Art materials that *are* designed for children have to meet stringent safety standards and are nontoxic. Take care to check labels of art and craft materials before purchasing to determine that they are nontoxic.

Snowflake Paintings

▶ **AGES:**
18 months to 4+ years

▶ **ACTIVITY TIME:**
10 to 20 minutes

Materials

- ◆ Ivory Snow Flakes
- ◆ water
- ◆ a wooden spoon, whisk, or eggbeater
- ◆ food coloring (optional)
- ◆ a brush*
- ◆ colored construction paper or other heavy paper to paint on
- ◆ newspaper, place mat, or plastic tray to paint on
- ◆ a smock or old adult-sized shirt for your child to wear (optional)

Activity

Mix one cup of Ivory Snow Flakes with about ⅛ cup water. Add the water gradually and stir until the flakes are the consistency of mashed potatoes. The white flakes can be used on black paper to make a night painting with snow, or add a few drops of food coloring to the mixture to create a smooth pastel color.

In Playspace, we like to mix two or three different colors of the Snow Flakes mixture and paint on light-colored paper. If you are using more than one color, use a brush for each color if possible. This keeps the colors from mixing together.

Encourage your child to move the paint around on the paper, using either her fingers or a brush to apply the paint to the paper. Keep a small cup of water on hand to stir into the paint in case it starts to get stiff.

*To make your own brush, see "How to Make a Paste and Paint Brush," p. 210.

What Your Child Is Learning	With this activity, your child is learning how to use a brush to make a variety of lines and shapes. This is a skill that takes time and practice to master. As she handles the oversized brush, she is developing valuable small motor skills that will eventually be refined. In time, these same skills will enable her to write her name and cut with scissors.
More Things to Do	
Paint with Water!	
Materials	♦ a sidewalk, driveway, or children's chalkboard easel ♦ a medium-sized plastic bowl or container ♦ a paintbrush, preferably with a long handle ♦ water ♦ a plastic tarp for the floor (if indoors) ♦ a smock or adult-sized shirt for your child to wear (optional)
Activity	Fill a bowl with 1 to 2 inches of water. Invite your child to paint with water on a hard, dry, porous surface, such as a sidewalk. Make long or short lines, wavy or straight. Paint circles and squares! Use some colored chalk along with the water painting. Write a "secret" message on a sunny day and watch while it magically disappears! A long-handled brush is easiest for your child to use for this kind of painting. All of the fun of painting, but without the mess!
Even More Things to Do	Finger-paint with shaving cream on a serving tray. You can add one drop of food coloring to the shaving cream for color. Don't forget a smock!

Fancy Finger Painting

▶ AGES:
12 months to 4+ years

▶ ACTIVITY TIME:
10 to 30 minutes

Materials:
- finger paint (from an art supply, craft and hobby, or educational supply store)
- finger paint paper (available in those same stores), or smooth, heavy paper such as freezer wrap paper
- a plastic place mat or newspaper to cover the work surface and extra newspaper to cover the floor
- a smock or old adult-sized shirt (optional)

Activity

Put out only a small amount of paint on the paper at a time. You can start with a spoonful a little bigger than a quarter. Encourage your child to feel the paint and spread it around on the paper. If the paper is moving around, tape it to the table.

For beginners, painting with one color is fine. For older children, painting with red, yellow, blue, white, and black will allow them to explore all of the possible color combinations.

What Your Child Is Learning

Finger painting is often a child's first painting experience. It is an opportunity for the child to explore paint without the small muscle coordination needed to handle a paintbrush. By showing your child that the marks he makes with his fingers are important, and through its use of bright colors, finger painting promotes both freedom of expression and your child's feelings of self-worth.

More Things to Do

Try using your fingernails or a plastic knife to draw and scratch in the paint.

Make hand or finger prints! Gently press your child's hand or fingers into the paint, then press them onto the paper.

With older children, try using finger paint for practicing letters or writing messages.

For parents with very young toddlers: Are you interested in finger painting but worried about the mess? Try having your child paint in a high chair with newspaper on the floor underneath. The high chair allows you to keep the activity and the cleanup contained and manageable.

Tempera Paintings

▶ AGES:	▶ ACTIVITY TIME:
18 months to 4+ years	**15 to about 35 minutes**

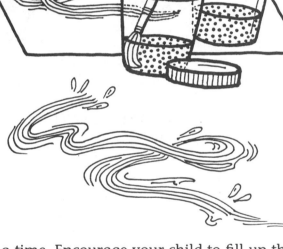

Materials

- ◆ tempera paint, powdered or premixed (available from an art, craft and hobby, or educational supply store)
- ◆ heavy paper, at least 8½ by 11 inches
- ◆ paint containers*, containers with lids, or Styrofoam trays
- ◆ brushes with short handles** (for tabletop painting)
- ◆ brushes with long handles (for easel painting)
- ◆ newspaper or plastic tarp to cover the work surface and floor
- ◆ a smock or an old adult-sized shirt for your child to wear (optional)

Activity

Put out only a small amount of paint at a time. Encourage your child to fill up the whole page. If he is tending to paint in only one spot, turn the paper around for him so that he has a clean space to paint on.

*See "How to Make a 'No-Spill' Paint Container," p. 211.
**To make your own brushes, see "How to Make a Paste or Paint Brush," p. 210.

For beginners, painting with one color is fine. For older children, painting with red, yellow, blue, white, and black will allow them to explore all of the possible color combinations. If possible, have a separate brush for each color so that the paint does not muddy quickly.

What Your Child Is Learning

Painting is immediate and gives children a sense of power and control. There is a sense of satisfaction that comes from making bold lines and sweeping curves. Playing with paint develops your child's imagination and bolsters self-esteem. Handling the brush uses eye-hand coordination and small motor skills.

More Things to Do

Mix colors to make new colors. When mixing, start with only a small amount of a lighter-colored paint and add a darker color a little bit at a time. An empty egg carton is perfect for experimenting.

Make a double painting! Have your child paint on one side of the paper, fold it in half, and rub the paper with his hand. What does he see when you open it up?

Create a "monoprint," or one-of-a-kind "print." Paint on a piece of Plexiglas, plastic tray, or place mat. Place a piece of paper over the painting while it is still wet, press down firmly, then lift.

Try painting with just a bowl of water and a brush. See "Paint with Water," p. 33, in the More Things to Do section.

▶ "Should I buy an easel?" An easel designed for preschoolers is a good investment if you plan on doing lots of art projects. Many easels come with a chalkboard on at least one side and can also be used for either drawing or displaying your child's finished artwork.

Rolling Ball Paintings

▶ **AGES:**
18 months to 4+ years

▶ **ACTIVITY TIME:**
15 to 30 minutes

Materials

- liquid tempera paint, 2 to 4 different colors (available at art supply, craft and hobby, and educational supply stores)
- a golf ball, or a plastic ball of a similar size and weight
- a brush*
- a small plastic tub or dishpan
- paper, about 8½ by 11 inches
- a small container of soapy water
- paper towels
- newspaper to cover the work surface, and extra newspaper for drying finished work
- a smock or old adult-sized shirt for your child to wear (optional)

Activity

Place a piece of paper inside of the dishpan. The paper should lie flat on the bottom.

If your paint came in a squeeze bottle, you can squeeze it right out of the bottle onto the ball. If your paint came in a jar, pour a very small amount into a paint container or sturdy cup. Dip the brush into the paint and brush a dollop about the size of a quarter onto the ball. Place the painted ball on top of the paper.

Ask your child to shake the container. The ball will roll over the paper and make lines according to his movements. Your child can practice sending the ball in different directions by tipping the container up and down and from side to side.

*To make your own brush, see "How to Make a Paste and Paint Brush," p. 210.

You can change paint colors as often as you like. Just dip the ball in soapy water and wipe it dry. Then brush on a new color.

What Your Child Is Learning

This activity uses unusual materials to create artwork. Finding new uses for everyday objects inspires creativity and creative problem solving in your child. The paint in this activity allows your child to watch the path of the ball. It is an interesting way to observe how round things roll and respond to changes in direction.

More Things to Do

Spin a painting! You need a clear plastic jar with a lid, a marble, paint, a brush, and a piece of paper. Place the paper inside the jar, wrapping it around the sides. Brush the paint onto the marble and add it to the jar. Close the lid and spin.

SPIN A PAINTING

Make marble paintings with children ages three and up. You need a shoe box with a lid, a marble, paper, paint, and a rubber band. Place the paper inside the box. Dip the marble in paint and add it to the box, replacing the lid. Secure the box with a rubber band. Shake!

Make a "road map." You'll need a small plastic car with moving tires. Dip the car into a little bit of paint and roll it across a piece of paper.

▶ Are you looking for a gift idea? This project creates beautiful results that look like faux marble finishes. Trim the painting with scissors to fit an inexpensive, ready-made frame. To frame it with a border, glue a complementary color of construction paper to the back of the painting. The construction paper should be slightly larger than the painting. If needed, trim the painting so that the edges of the construction paper show.

MARBLE PAINTINGS

Sponge Printing

► AGES:
18 months to 4+ years

► ACTIVITY TIME:
5 to 15 minutes

Materials

- tempera paint, powdered or premixed (available from art supply, craft and hobby, and educational supply stores)
- kitchen sponges or foam pieces
- scissors
- a utility knife for cutting more complicated shapes (optional)
- heavy paper, at least 8½ by 11 inches
- paintbrushes, one for each color if possible
- Styrofoam trays or disposable pie tins for paint
- clothespins
- a smock or old adult-sized shirt for your child to wear (optional)
- newspaper, plastic tray, or place mat to use as a work surface, and extra newspaper for drying finished work

Activity

Ahead of time, use scissors to cut pieces of sponge into simple shapes, such as triangles, squares, half-moons, and hearts. Once they have been cut, attach clothespins to the center of the sponge pieces. Your child can use the clothespin like a handle when she's painting.

Next, brush a thin layer of paint on a Styrofoam tray or pie tin. For beginners and young toddlers, printing with just one or two colors is fine. With children two and older, it is nice to have a range of colors available.

The paint tray is used like an ink pad. Dip a shape into the paint and then press it onto the paper. For best results, place a cushion of newspaper underneath your child's paper.

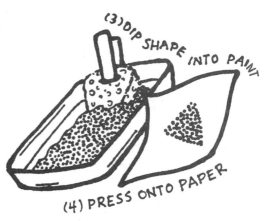

(3) DIP SHAPE INTO PAINT

(4) PRESS ONTO PAPER

What Your Child Is Learning

This project is simple and immediate. Children do not need special skills to participate. Your child feels successful because she can manipulate the stamps easily and the finished product always looks nice. The stamps used in this project give young children practice identifying simple shapes. Older children can use these simple shapes to invent patterns.

More Things to Do

Just for parents: Make some homemade stamps! Mount some of your foam shapes onto a small block of wood for longer use. This is a great idea for seasonal or holiday designs. Use a glue or epoxy that is not water soluble, so that your stamps won't fall apart the next time you paint.

Print with old kitchen gadgets! Forks, spoons, and potato mashers make interesting prints. Yard sales and secondhand stores are some of the places where you can buy these items inexpensively.

What's in your toolbox? Washers, nuts, and bolts can be a lot of fun to print with. These items are not recommended for use with children under three.

Printing with Fruits and Vegetables

▶ **AGES:**
18 months to 4+ years

▶ **ACTIVITY TIME:**
10 to 30 minutes

Materials

- ♦ fruits and vegetables—apples, pears, green peppers, and onions
- ♦ tempera paint, either powdered or premixed (available at art supply, craft and hobby, and educational supply stores)
- ♦ heavy paper, at least 8½ by 11 inches
- ♦ Styrofoam trays or disposable pie tins
- ♦ paintbrushes, one for each color if possible
- ♦ a kitchen knife
- ♦ newspaper, plastic tray, or place mat to print on, and extra newspaper for drying finished work
- ♦ a smock or old adult-sized shirt for your child to wear (optional)

Activity

Cut fruits and vegetables in half through the center or core.

With a brush, paint a thin layer of paint onto a Styrofoam tray or pie tin. This way, if the tray is knocked over while your child is painting, there won't be a mess.

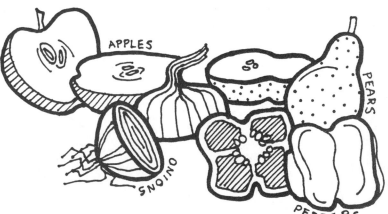

Using the paint tray like an ink pad, press the fruit pieces into the paint and then onto the paper. For best results, cushion your child's paper with a layer of newspaper.

The primary colors—red, blue, and yellow—are recommended for printing. Beginners may start with only one or two of these colors. For children three and up, this activity is also an opportunity to learn about how colors interact, so having color choices becomes important.

What Your Child Is Learning

Printing with fruits and vegetables is a way for your child to take a close look at things that he eats every day. He can see that onions are made up of many layers, that apples have lots of flesh and a core with seeds, and that green peppers look very different on the inside and the outside. This activity encourages observation skills and an interest in how things grow.

More Things to Do

Print a star! Cut an apple in half lengthwise, so that the stem is part of one half and the bottom of the apple is part of the other. The core of the apple in cross-section looks like a star.

Add variation to your prints. Use colored construction paper for background paper. Paint colors look different depending on the color of the background. Compare blue paint on white paper to blue paint on orange paper.

Print with broccoli or corn on the cob! With older kids, wash off the vegetables and look at them with a magnifying glass. Talk about what you see.

> ► Make your child feel special! Print his fingerprints by gently pressing his fingers into an ink pad and then onto a piece of paper. Tell him that no one else has fingerprints exactly like his. With older kids, use a magnifying glass to look at and compare fingerprints.

Printing with String

Materials

To Make String Blocks
- ◆ standard household string or yarn
- ◆ small wooden blocks or wood scraps (plan on having one string block for each color you are using)

To Print
- ◆ tempera paint, either powdered or premixed (available at art supply, craft and hobby, and educational supply stores)
- ◆ Styrofoam trays or disposable pie tins
- ◆ paintbrushes, one for each color if possible
- ◆ heavy paper, at least 8½ by 11 inches
- ◆ scissors
- ◆ newspaper, plastic tray, or place mat to print on, and extra newspaper for drying finished work
- ◆ a smock or old adult-sized shirt for your child to wear (optional)

Activity

To Make a Block
Tie a long piece of string to one end of a wooden block. Wrap the remaining string around the block to create an interesting design. The string can be

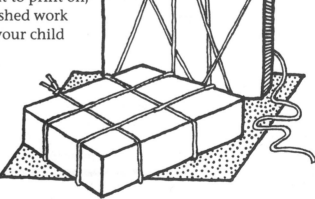

wrapped in a variety of patterns, including a square grid, vertical lines, a sunburst shape, or an asymmetrical design.

To Print
With a brush, place a thin layer of paint on a Styrofoam tray or pie tin. For beginners and young toddlers, painting with one color of paint is recommended as a convenient way of minimizing mess. It is nice to have at least three colors available for older children.

To make a print, dip the wooden block into the paint tray and then press in onto your paper. The design from the raised string will create a design on your child's paper. Paint colors stay pure if you use one block per color. For best results, cushion your child's paper with a layer of newspaper.

What Your Child Is Learning

This activity emphasizes experimentation with pattern and color. Pattern is a combination of line, color, and shape and is an important visual element. The ease with which your child can manipulate these patterns makes her feel successful. The practice arranging patterns and colors on a page develops her creative and esthetic sensibilities.

More Things to Do

Make a callograph! A callograph is a printing technique where raised objects create texture. Glue pasta, yarn, cardboard shapes, and other textural objects to a piece of cardboard. Allow the glue to dry thoroughly. Brush on tempera paint, lay a piece of paper on top, and rub with the palm of your hand. Peel off to reveal your print.

See "How to Make Easy Potato Stamps," p. 217.

Beautiful Dyed Paper

► AGES:
18 months to 4+ years

► ACTIVITY TIME:
5 to 20 minutes

Materials

- three small plastic bowls filled with 1 to 2 inches of water
- red, yellow, and blue food coloring
- coffee filters for a drip coffeemaker (twenty filters will make ten dyed pieces)
- lots of newspaper to cover the work surface and to place underneath drying pieces

Activity

Use newspaper to create an out-of-the-way spot where the dyed coffee filters can dry. Separate the coffee filters into sets of two. Doubling the filters will give you better dyeing results.

Add ten to fifteen drops of either red, yellow, or blue food coloring to each bowl of water and stir. These colors are recommended because they create the broadest range of colors when they are combined.

Before you start, test the colors to see if they are ready to use by dipping a corner of the coffee filter into each one. If the dye on the filter is very pale, add more food coloring, three to five drops at a time, until the color looks vibrant on the filter paper.

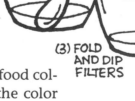

(1) ADD FOOD COLOR

(2) STIR

(3) FOLD AND DIP FILTERS

Next, crinkle or fold the paper. Your child can do this any way she likes. The key to success is not in the folding, it's in the dipping. Dip only a portion of your paper into a bowl. Next, dip another portion into the second bowl, and so on. Squeeze out the filter between dips. It is best to start with the lightest color and move toward the darkest. This keeps the colors from turning brown.

For another effect, fill an eyedropper with dye and squeeze it directly on to the coffee filter.

What Your Child Is Learning

This activity involves playing with colors. It introduces your child to primary and secondary colors. The primary colors are red, yellow, and blue. All other colors stem from their combinations. Secondary colors are created by mixing two primary colors, like blue and yellow for green or red and blue for purple. Older children can explore how variations in folding yield different designs.

More Things to Do

Try different ways of folding and crinkling the filters. What happens if you fold the filter up like a paper fan? What about a triangle shape?

Cut up the dyed filters into shapes and use the pieces to make cards and collages.

Make a paper flower! Once the dyed filters are dry, lay two or three of them together. Pinch the paper in the center of the circles and twist with your fingers. Secure to a pipe cleaner with a rubber band. Experiment with trimming the edges of the circles to make different petal shapes. It is easiest to do this before you put the flower together.

For older children, ages three and up: Be a scientist. Do an experiment to see what colors are in a marker! Draw a dot with a marker (black is a good color to start with) on a coffee filter or white paper napkin. With an eyedropper or a straw, let water droplets fall onto the mark, one at a time. Watch what happens to the dot. How many different colors do you see?

> Are you looking for a project that works equally well for older and younger kids? This activity suits a wide range of ages. Toddlers like seeing the colors and older children keep busy devising more complicated folding techniques. Best of all, the results are always impressive.

CHAPTER 2

Science Is Fun

Play Dough Recipes

► AGES:
12 months to 4+ years

► ACTIVITY TIME:
5 to 25 minutes

Marcy's Cooked Play Dough

Although this recipe is more involved than the uncooked version, the play dough stores well and can be used again and again. Ready to use ten minutes after cooking, the consistency of this recipe is like the store-bought version.

Materials

- 1½ cups flour
- ¾ cup salt
- 1 tablespoon cream of tartar
- 3 tablespoons vegetable oil
- 1½ cups water
- a wooden spoon
- 2 medium-sized bowls
- a few drops of food coloring (optional)

Recipe

Mix the dry ingredients.

In a separate bowl, mix the wet ingredients, including the food coloring.

Combine the wet and dry ingredients. Stir.

Cook the ingredients over low heat on the stove, stirring constantly, until dough is the consistency of thickened mashed potatoes.

Cool and store in a zip-seal bag. Place the bag in a coffee can or airtight plastic container.

Note: It's fun to do it together! Your child can help with the first three steps of this recipe. If she is too young to measure or pour the ingredients, put the mixture in a large bowl and ask her to help you stir the mixture.

Uncooked Play Dough

This recipe is quick and simple—you can whip up some dough at a moment's notice. The play dough from this recipe feels great to use but does not store well. Plan on using it just for one play session.

This dough can also be dried and baked to a hard finish. Use it for projects that you would like to keep. To harden the dough, bake at 300 degrees for ten to fifteen minutes. After cooling, projects can be painted with watercolor or tempera paints.

Materials

- 1 cup of flour
- ¼ cup of salt
- ½ cup of water
- a few drops of food coloring (optional)
- a wooden spoon
- a medium-sized bowl

Recipe

Combine the dry ingredients.
Add food coloring to the water.
Add water slowly to the dry mixture. Stir with a spoon until partially mixed.
Knead dough.

Ask your child to help you mix the play dough. He can help you measure the ingredients, stir and knead the dough. To involve a younger child, you can fill the measuring cup and let him add the contents to the bowl.

Recipe Tip: It usually takes a few tries to get a feel for mixing the play dough to the right consistency. Add the water slowly, as sometimes a batch will use slightly less than the ½ cup called for in the recipe.

The dough should be firm and not sticky. If you find that you have used too much water, add small amounts of flour and salt to reconstitute the dough. Continue kneading until the play dough becomes firm.

Play Dough Play

▶ **AGES:**
12 months to 4+ years

▶ **ACTIVITY TIME:**
5 to 30 minutes

Materials
- ♦ "Play Dough" (see recipes, pp. 50–51)
- ♦ a countertop, place mat, or plastic tray to use as a work surface
- ♦ any of the following items (optional): cookie cutters, rolling pins, a wooden meat tenderizer, a plastic knife, rubber stamps, children's scissors

Activity

Play dough is an activity that involves all of the senses. Encourage your child to smell it, feel it, even taste it. Talk about the ingredients used in the recipe and how they change when they are combined.

Play dough can be used on its own or with tools like cookie cutters or rolling pins. It can be shaped and reshaped again and again. Your child can pound it, pull it, cut it, and roll it to her heart's content.

Special creations can be saved when using the "uncooked" recipe. Allow the pieces to air-dry, and paint them later on with watercolor or tempera paints if you wish.

What Your Child Is Learning

Your child is learning that simple household ingredients can be combined to create "dough." She is forming and shaping a mass of material. She learns that soft material can be manipulated, imprinted, shaped, cut, or rolled. Rolling makes things thinner. Scissors and cookie cutters make shapes. A ball of play dough can be anything your child wishes; there is an unlimited capacity for creative discovery.

More Things to Do

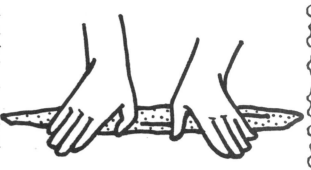

With ages three and up: Roll play dough "snakes." Show your child how to roll a length of dough with the palms of her hands to create a long coil or "snake." Start with your palms together in the center of the dough, rolling away from you. Slowly work your hands out toward the ends. Repeat until the dough is the desired thickness.

Use a garlic press to make lots of long, skinny spaghetti. A wonderful trick for making "hair" on projects with older kids.

Mix two batches of different-colored play dough. Roll the colors together for a "marbled" effect.

> ▶ *Does your child have a short attention span?*
>
> Play dough is a tactile activity that can help focus children who tend to have short attention spans. Give it a try!
>
> ▶ *What is problem solving and why is it important?*
>
> Problem solving is important because it is a measure of your child's ability to take apart a problem and come up with a workable solution. The problem can be as simple as "How can we flatten this ball of play dough? We could roll it. With what? A rolling pin. Okay, let's try it. Look, it's working! What else could we do to it? Pound it?" And so on.

Cool Color Trays

Materials

- ◆ one or two white plastic ice cube trays
- ◆ an eyedropper
- ◆ a cup of water
- ◆ red, yellow, and blue food coloring
- ◆ warm water

Activity

Ask your child to help you fill the ice cube tray half full with lukewarm water. White trays work best because it is easy to see the colors that you are mixing against a white background.

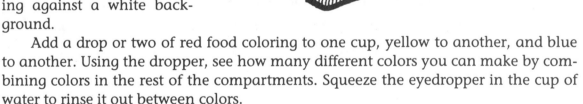

Add a drop or two of red food coloring to one cup, yellow to another, and blue to another. Using the dropper, see how many different colors you can make by combining colors in the rest of the compartments. Squeeze the eyedropper in the cup of water to rinse it out between colors.

Ask your child what two colors combine to make green. Can he name some other things that are green?

Try using colors to "paint" pictures with the eyedropper on white paper towels or absorbent paper.

What Your Child Is Learning

Your child is learning about the science of color theory. He is experimenting with color mixing to create color combinations and see how certain colors are derived. The colors that he begins with are the primary colors, the roots of all color combinations. The colors that are created when red, yellow, and blue are combined are the secondary colors. Ask him, "How many colors can you mix using the color red?"

More Things to Do

After you've mixed the colors, place a Popsicle stick in two or three compartments and place the tray in the freezer. The popsicle stick doesn't need to be straight for it to work. When the "colors" are frozen, use these "colored brushes" to paint a picture on thick white paper, such as freezer wrap.

Read a story about color mixing, such as *Mouse Paint* by Ellen Stoll Walsh (Red Wagon Books, 1995).

▶ *"I have an eighteen-month-old and she can't do some of these activities. Why are they recommended for such young kids?"*

We recommend that parents try these activities with their children at an early age to begin their exposure to materials and ideas that will become important to them later on. An eighteen-month-old may spend only a minute or two with an activity before losing interest or need a parent's help to participate. Nevertheless, over time this repeated short exposure will help build her attention span, problem-solving skills, coordination, and self-esteem.

The Sun Rises

Begin the poem sitting in a cross-legged position.

Poem and Movements

The sun rises in the morning	(raise your arms from the center of your body)
And spreads its light	(open your arms to the sides and down to the floor)
From one side	(lean from the waist to the right, right arm to the floor, left arm stretches over head)
To the other side	(lean from the waist to the left, left arm on the floor, right arm over head)
And then it goes to sleep behind a cloud	(place your head down with your arms over it)
The moon rises	(raise your body and place your hands over your face)
And shows its face	(open your hands and remove them from your face and smile)

What Your Child Is Learning

This poem teaches basic science concepts about the sun and the moon. The motions work on motor skills and flexibility.

Bathing Babies

▶ AGES:
12 months to 4+ years

▶ ACTIVITY TIME:
10 to 30 minutes

Materials

- ◆ a plastic baby doll
- ◆ two plastic dish tubs
- ◆ a small sponge or a washcloth
- ◆ baby shampoo to make soapsuds
- ◆ a bath mat for the floor
- ◆ a towel
- ◆ a diaper and doll clothes (for after bath)
- ◆ a baby powder shaker (or an empty one for pretend)
- ◆ a smock or apron for your child to wear (optional)

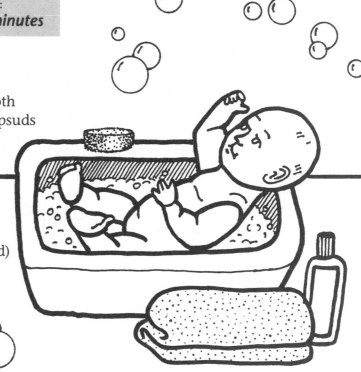

Activity

Fill one of the tubs with 1 to 2 inches of warm water. Add some baby shampoo to make suds. Fill the other tub with clean water for rinsing. Set up the tubs on a low table with the bath mat underneath.

Let your child play in the water, then introduce the baby doll. Children twelve to eighteen months old won't be able to follow a strict sequence, but will enjoy playing freely with the doll in the water. With an older child, show her how to undress, wash, and shampoo the baby. Then rinse, dry, diaper, and dress the doll.

Talk to your child about the order in which things happen. What should we do first? What comes next? Now the baby is clean and dry, what should we do now?

Read the "baby" a story or sing a song after the bath.

What Your Child Is Learning

"Bathing Babies" gives your child a chance to demonstrate what she knows about cleanliness and hygiene. Water, soap, and a little bit of scrubbing get things clean. Often, with this activity, the science involved is secondary to the allure of the pretend element. "Bathing Babies" gives your child the opportunity to play an adult role in a familiar setting and in the process, satisfies her impulse to try on the role of the caretaker.

More Things to Do

Give your child some props to play with that you use around the house. With a set of play keys or a blanket and pillow, she can take the baby for a ride or put the baby to sleep after its bath.

For another washing activity, try washing the dishes with plastic cups, plates, and containers. Recycled yogurt containers or Tupperware are perfect.

▶ *Are you looking for ways to prepare your child for a new baby?*

Parent quote: "Bathing Babies was Kelly's favorite activity when I was pregnant. She asked for it each time we went to Playspace. Washing babies let her be loving and practice how she would be able to help Mom and Dad when the new baby came."

It is important for young children to have a chance to show that although they are usually the ones being cared for, they are also capable of nurturing behavior.

Real (No Kidding) Fish Prints

▶ AGES:
2 to 4+ years

▶ ACTIVITY TIME:
15 to 30 minutes

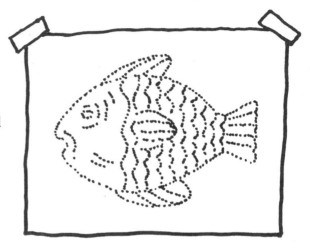

Materials

- tempera paint, powdered or premixed (we recommend black)
- a whole fish that has not been cleaned or gutted
- a Styrofoam tray
- heavy paper, at least 8½ by 11 inches
- a mat or newspaper to print on
- extra newspaper for the floor
- paintbrushes

Activity

Prepare the work surface. Rinse the fish with warm water and pat it dry with a paper towel.

Place the fish on a Styrofoam tray and ask your child to brush it with a thin layer of paint. The thinner the paint is, the more detail will show up on the print. Be careful of the scales. Once the fish has been painted, remove it from the tray and place it on a clean piece of newspaper for printing.

Next, place a piece of paper over the fish and encourage your child to pat it down firmly all over with the palm of her hand, including the head and the tail. Peel the paper off slowly; you should have a detailed imprint of the fish, including the scales and fins.

If the paint is too thick, you may not get a good print. If this happens, place another piece of paper over the fish and repeat the printing process again, without adding more paint. Continue printing with new paper until the print shows the desired detail. Also, you can try thinning the paint slightly with water.

The fish is still edible after printing, should you wish to prepare it. Wash it well with warm water to remove the paint. Tempera paints are nontoxic.

What Your Child Is Learning

"Fish Prints" give your child the opportunity to have an intimate look at an animal that lives in the water. It is a lesson in biology: she can see and touch the fish's fins, scales, and tail. Experiences that bring her in close contact with the natural world build her appreciation for living things and the environment.

More Things to Do

Make a fish shirt! Print your fish with a water-based fabric paint on a white T-shirt.

Print with fruits and vegetables like apples, pears, green peppers, or potatoes! Cut them in half and brush them with paint. For more information, see "Printing with Fruits and Vegetables," p. 42.

▶ Fish printing is an ancient Japanese art form known as *gyotaku*. Prints are traditionally done with black ink on rice paper.

Go Fishing! Magnet Magic

Materials

- fish shapes cut from construction or heavy paper
- markers or crayons (optional)
- a hole punch
- large paper clips
- a paper towel roll
- string
- scissors
- small magnets that you can tie a string to securely (available at toy or educational supply stores):
    - a doughnut-shaped magnet or other shaped magnets
    - U-shaped magnet
    - bar magnet
- a wide, shallow cardboard box (you can paint it blue for effect), blue sheet, or small plastic baby pool to use as a pond

Activity

To Make the Fish

Cut out fish shapes ahead of time from pieces of heavy paper. Punch a hole near the mouth area on each fish and loop a paper clip through the hole. Attach a few more paper clips to the first one to make a chain. The fish may be decorated with markers or crayons. Place all of the fish in the "water."

To Make the Fishing Pole

Punch two holes in the paper towel roll, about 1 inch from one end, one hole on either side. Thread a long piece of string through both of the holes. Tie the string to itself to make a knot at one end. Tie a magnet to the other end of the string. Your child is now ready to catch some fish.

Go Fishing

Show her how to use her pole to attract the paper clips on the fish. She can cast around and slowly lift the fish out of the water. How many can she catch at once?

What else will her fishing pole catch? Put other household items into the "water" and see which ones she can catch. Experiment with spoons or other kitchen utensils, metal toys, coins, pencils, erasers, dice, plastic toys, tinfoil, or even other magnets. Find out which items are attracted to magnets and which are not.

What Your Child Is Learning

With a little ingenuity, games can be used to teach weighty concepts in a way that is engaging for children. "Go Fishing" is a learning experience that will introduce your child to magnets. She will experience magnets' special pull. She will see that some objects are attracted and will "stick" to the magnet. As she fishes for household items, she discovers that other objects are not affected by magnets.

More Things to Do

Play with some magnetic letters on the refrigerator. Can you help your child to spell her full name?

Design your own refrigerator magnet! You'll need magnetic backing from a craft store. It is sold in strips. Cut some simple shapes from lightweight cardboard. Have your child decorate the cardboard with drawing or collage materials and glue it to the magnetic backing with epoxy or other bonding glue.

> ▶ *But I don't know anything about science!*
>
> Lots of adults feel they don't have strong science backgrounds, but you don't need to be a physicist to create lively science experiences for your child. Science is really about being an active learner, someone who is inquisitive about the world and how it works.

Crayon Resist

▶ AGES:
3 to 4+ years

▶ ACTIVITY TIME:
15 to 25 minutes

Materials

- crayons
- watercolors or tempera paint (available from art supply, craft and hobby, and educational supply stores)
- brushes*
- a paint container**
- heavy paper, such as manila or construction paper, in light colors, at least 8½ by 11 inches
- newspaper, place mat, or plastic tray to paint on
- a smock or old adult-sized shirt for your child to wear (optional)

Activity

Prepare the work surface. Ask your child to draw a picture using crayons. The more bright colors and details he uses, the better the final results will be. Remember to leave some blank space on the paper for the painting part of the project.

When the drawing is done, paint over the whole picture, including your child's crayon drawing. Wipe up excess paint with a paper towel or damp sponge. Soon the

*See "How to Make a Paste and Paint Brush," p. 210.
**See "How to Make a 'No-Spill' Paint Container," p. 211.

"science" part of the project will become evident. Your child's crayon drawing has not been erased. The wax in the crayon creates a "resist," which doesn't allow the wet paint to penetrate it.

What Your Child Is Learning

Your child is learning that crayons and paint together create a unique picture. He is exploring color, different artistic mediums, and how they can be combined.

More Things to Do

Make an underwater picture! Color a picture of sea life. Paint over it with blue paint!

Make an "antique" picture. Draw a picture with crayons, covering as much of the paper as possible. Crumple it up into a ball. Open it back up and flatten it out. Paint it with a dark color of tempera paint, like black. The paint will get into the cracks of the picture and make it look old. Wipe off excess paint with a paper towel.

Bird Feeder

> ▶ **AGES:**
> **2 years to 4+ years**
> **(younger children enjoy**
> **these bird feeders, but**
> **need lots of adult help)**
>
> ▶ **ACTIVITY TIME:**
> **10 to 20 minutes**

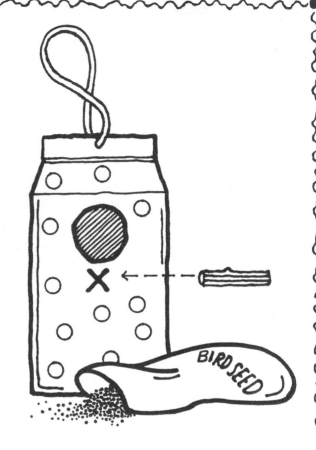

Materials

- an empty milk carton, either paper or plastic, one pint or larger (remember to rinse it out beforehand)
- a utility knife or scissors
- a stick, 4 to 6 inches long
- yarn, string, or fishing line
- birdseed
- decorating materials (optional), such as:
  file folder stickers (dots), but any stickers will do
  colored tissue, applied with a brush and a glue-and-water mixture
- polyurethane or other acrylic coating to preserve decorations, either in a spray can or for use with a brush
- newspaper for the work surface if you are decorating

Activity

To Make the Bird Feeder

First, use scissors or a utility knife to cut a round hole in one side of the milk carton. The hole should be three inches in diameter. Place the hole in the center of the carton, about a third of the way up. This is where the birds will feed.

Next, make two small slits in the shape of an X underneath the center of the hole. Leave about ³/₄ inch of space between the hole and the X.

Finally, if your milk jug does not have a handle, poke a hole in the middle of the top lip of the carton. The hole should be large enough for a piece of string to slide through. Now your child is ready to help you with the rest of the construction.

Slide the stick through the X you made, so that it juts out from the carton. This will be the bird's perch. Tie a long piece of string to your milk carton, either to the handle or through the hole that you made in the top.

If you wish to add decorations to your bird feeder, see the "To Decorate" section.

Once the feeder has been constructed and decorated, it is ready to be filled with birdseed. Find a good viewing spot and hang it where you can watch the birds come and go.

To Decorate (optional)
Note: Decorate before you fill the feeder.

Your child can decorate the feeder to make it more attractive. Dot stickers from file folders are a fast, clean, and colorful way to decorate, although the color will fade a little with time.

A longer process, but one that yields beautiful results, is to collage with colored tissue and watered-down white glue. Mix three parts white glue to two parts water. The glue should be thin enough to be spread with a brush. Simply hold a piece of tissue in place and paint over it with the mixture. The color combinations that can be created with this project are phenomenal. Have lots of newspaper on hand for this one, because the glue mixture is runny.

To preserve the colors of the tissue so that they don't run together once it has been hung, we recommend some type of acrylic fixative, such as polyurethane. Many brands are available in a spray can or small can to use with a brush. This fixative should be used by an adult only, outside or in a well-ventilated place in accordance with the instructions on the packaging.

What Your Child Is Learning

Watching birds feed is both a fascinating and calming activity for all ages. What do birds eat? How many different birds come to the feeder? How do you tell the males from the females? Having a bird feeder is an excellent way to connect your child to the environment around him and show him how his generosity can benefit wildlife.

More Things to Do

A natural fall feeder: Roll a pine cone first in peanut butter, then in birdseed. Tie a string to the top and hang it up outside. Who comes to eat?

Go on a bird-watching walk! Do you have any binoculars? How many different birds do you see? Take out a bird book from the library and learn the names of some birds that live in your area.

CHAPTER 3

Things to Do Outside

Blowing Bubbles

▶ AGES:	▶ ACTIVITY TIME:
12 months to 4+ years	*5 to 30 minutes*

Materials

- ◆ a plastic container
- ◆ bubble solution: liquid dishwashing soap and water
- ◆ bubble-making tools: plastic wands, plastic berry baskets, a spatula, plastic cups with the bottoms cut off, plastic plates with a hole cut in the center, paper towel and toilet paper rolls, bubble wands (instructions below)

Activity

Mix one part liquid soap to three parts water. Joy has the most glycerin, which is the key ingredient for bubbles. You can also add a touch of corn syrup to make the bubbles last longer.

Experiment with a variety of wands and tools to blow bubbles. Blow one large bubble or lots of small bubbles. Younger children can catch and pop the bubbles you blow. Older children can learn to blow their own bubbles while you hold the wand.

Stick a wet straw into a bubble. The bubble will not break. Can you repeat that trick with a wet finger?

Learn how to blow a bubble without a wand. First, wet your hands thoroughly. Next, place both of your thumbs and both of your forefingers together to form a diamond shape. Keeping your fingers together, dip your hands into the bubble solution. Lift them out slowly and blow.

Look at a bubble up close. How many colors do you see?

What Your Child Is Learning

Bubbles are enchanting. They shimmer in sunlight and are so light that they float with the breeze. Some scientists study bubbles to understand concepts like molecular structure and air-supported structures. Blowing and catching bubbles is sheer fun for all ages, but the forces behind their creation are serious science.

More Things to Do

Use an empty juice can to make big bubbles. Remember to smooth the can's rough edges with sandpaper before you use it.

How to Make Bubble Wands

For ages two to four years and up.

Materials

- ♦ string, 36 inches long
- ♦ two straws (if you are using bendable straws, cut off the part that bends)
- ♦ scissors
- ♦ a small plastic container to hold the solution

Directions

Thread the string through the two straws. Tie the ends of the string together. The straws form the "handles" for this bubble tool. Adults and older children can use this wand on their own, but younger children will probably need some help.

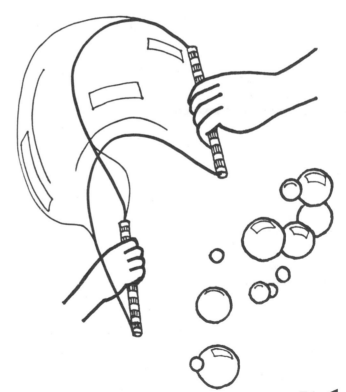

Activity

Dip the wand into the soap solution. Demonstrate for your child how the wand works before you try it together. Hold on to both ends of the wand with the straw handles. Lift the wand gently out of the water. Raise the wand with an upward motion, bringing your hands together. This motion will release a large bubble.

Now try it with your child. Hold on to one of the straw handles and ask your child to hold on to the other side. Coordinating your movements will take some practice. Do not stir up the bubble solution before trying this activity. Scoop off any foam resting on the surface of the water before you begin.

Can you use the same building technique to make a triangular wand? What shaped bubble does the triangle make?

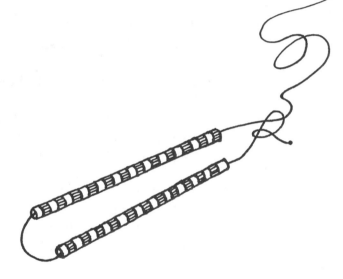

Where do all of the colors in a bubble come from?

The colors that you see in a bubble are the colors present in light rays, which bend when they hit the surface of the bubble. As the light rays bend, the light is broken up and all of their colors are visible. The principle is the same one that makes a rainbow or a prism so spectacular.

Bubble trouble shooting. If your bubble solution isn't working:
Are there a lot of suds on the surface? If so, scoop them out. You don't have to keep stirring the bubble mixture for it to work. Too much stirring can actually make it harder to blow bubbles.

If your soap solution still isn't working:
Add more liquid soap in small increments until it passes the following test. Hold your two thumbs and two forefingers together and make a diamond shape with your hands. Dip your hands into the bubble solution. If a soap film forms on your hands when you lift them from the solution, the soap ratio is correct.

Planting a Climbing Garden

▶ AGES:
2 to 4+ years

▶ ACTIVITY TIME:
15 to 20 minutes

Materials

- a planting pot, either round or window-box shaped
  (Choose a fairly large round pot, so that the seeds have room to grow. Pots can be either plastic or clay. Plastic is less expensive.)
- morning glory seeds
- potting soil (you can buy bags with 90 days of fertilizer added to the mix)
- a trowel
- a pair of work gloves
- drainage material for the bottom of the potting container, any of the following: gravel, Styrofoam packing peanuts, broken pieces of a clay planting pot, Styrofoam meat trays or take-out containers (rinsed and broken into pieces)
- two or three wooden gardening stakes or tall, thin sticks of any height
- a watering can or hose with a spray nozzle
- a hammer and large nail (if your container does not have drainage holes in the bottom)

Activity

First, make sure that the container you have chosen has proper drainage holes in the bottom. Some plastic window boxes do not come with holes for drainage. If this is the case, punch two or three holes in the bottom of your container with a hammer and large nail. Three holes—one hole at either end and a hole in the middle—should be sufficient.

Along with your child, fill the bottom of the planting pot with about 2 inches of drainage material. This will ensure that the water can exit the container and will prevent the roots of your plants from rotting. Choose from the materials listed above,

such as gravel, Styrofoam, etc. Place a nice, thick layer of potting soil over the drainage material.

Check the back of the seed packet to see what the suggested depth and spacing are for your seeds. Fill the container with potting soil, leaving enough space to plant your seeds at the suggested depth. Mark the spacing for the seeds by pressing your finger into the soil. Ask your child to place a seed at each place you marked in the dirt. Try not to place the seeds too close together. If you do end up with a clump of seedlings, you can always spread them out later on, while they are still young plants.

Once you have finished planting, water the seeds, so that they can begin to grow. Show your child how to water from either a can or a hose. Start with a watering can that is only partially full of water or a hose turned to a very fine spray. You can show your child how to water a little and then wait until the water has been absorbed before watering again. Keep the seeds moist while they are germinating. Morning glories are very hardy, so you do not need to worry about neglecting them once they have sprouted.

Morning glories like to have something to climb on. Once your seeds begin to sprout, place a few gardening stakes into the potting container so that they have something to wrap around. Once they are tall enough, show your child how to wrap them gently around the garden stakes. The morning glories will quickly master the stakes and be ready for greater climbing feats. Place the container near stair or deck railings, porch columns, or lattice and watch them climb up. When the vines reach the right height, "train" them by gently wrapping them around the railings or lattice.

It is fun to train your morning glories to climb up lengths of string. You can start training them onto the string after they have climbed onto the gardening stakes.

Place the container next to the side of your house, or porch. Tie a piece of string to the top of each gardening stake. Stretch the pieces of string either vertically or horizontally. Place a nail into a piece of the wooden trim on your home, or around a window frame, door frame, or porch column. Tie the remaining end of the string to the nail.

Morning glories are a great first planting experience. They are fast growing, their climbing action is exciting to watch, and their flowers are large and beautifully colored. It is fascinating to watch them open and close each day. Plus, they are hardy and can stand up to overwatering by zealous little gardeners.

Please note: Morning glory seeds need to be soaked in water overnight before planting. Always supervise small children while planting to make sure that they do not ingest any seeds.

What Your Child Is Learning

Planting seeds and watching them grow is one of the beautiful things in life. Flowers require consistent attention and a gentle touch in order to grow. Planting and cultivating seeds is a calming activity that offers a young child a real sense of being responsible for the care of a living thing.

More Things to Do

What else can you grow? Start another container with marigolds or nasturtiums.

If you have a sunny patch of ground, plant some sunflowers and see which one grows the tallest.

Pick some flower blooms and press them between pages in a phone book.

Playing with Water

▶ AGES:
12 months to 4+ years

▶ ACTIVITY TIME:
5 to 35 minutes

Materials

- a wading pool, large dishpan, plastic tub, or commercial water table*
- towels and aprons or smocks for your child to wear
- choose from the following:
  plastic or rubber toys
  plastic cups and bowls, empty yogurt containers, shampoo or bottles for liquid dishwashing soap, etc.
  a sponge (can be cut into small pieces)
  a small washcloth
  baby shampoo to make suds
- a few drops of food coloring (optional)

Activity

Fill the container with 1½ to 2 inches of water. Make sure that you both have on clothes that you don't mind getting wet.

*A commercial water table is a low, rectangular table with holes cut out for dishtub-sized pans. The low height and spill-proof design of these tables makes them a convenient choice for water or sand play. They are available through educational supply stores.

Place the play items within reach of your child. He can use cups and bowls for filling and pouring, play with some rubber toys, and use the sponge to wipe up. Let him investigate some of the possibilities and follow his lead.

Add a few drops of food coloring to the water for color. It makes it easier for your child to see what he's doing. Or, set two tubs with different colors next to each other. Try yellow and blue or red and blue. Mix and pour!

Wash the dishes! Let your child wash some plastic plates, glasses, or silverware. Good habits start early! Use a tub of soapy water for washing and a tub of clean water to rinse. Don't forget the dish rack and dish towel.

Water play can be messy and wet, but to young children it means endless play and a chance to use their imagination.

What Your Child Is Learning

Playing with water gives your child a hands-on look at the properties of water: what it looks like, how it pours, and how it can be contained. He is learning about the difference between wet and dry, and about the concepts of measuring, floating, and sinking.

More Things to Do

Use a funnel! Ask your child to place his hand underneath the funnel while you pour water into the spout. He will see that the funnel is open at both ends and that water

---

▶ *How do I steer the activity in a new direction?*

You can always say, "Alex, look at this!" But leave the choice up to him. If he is absorbed in an activity, provided it is not disruptive, he is getting something out of it, no matter how repetitious it may seem. As adults, we tend to forget the fascination of discovery. Our need to keep moving may inadvertently result in rushing a child through an activity. Take a deep breath and be patient!

can flow through it. Show your child how to fill the container by pouring water into the funnel. Pour water into containers with both wide and narrow mouths. Pour water fast and pour it slow. Children love funnels because they don't expect a container to be open at both ends. It is fascinating for children to watch how the funnel shapes and directs the flow of water.

Show your child how a sponge works.

Try "Playing with Water" inside at bath time or at the kitchen sink. Water play is possible in any room of the house, provided you use a small tub and only a little bit of water. A plastic tarp will protect the floor.

Floating and Sinking

▶ AGES:
2 to 4 + years

▶ ACTIVITY TIME:
10 to 30 minutes

Materials

- Select both heavy and light objects from the following:
  small toys like boats, play people, animals
  small plastic containers, cups and bowls, spoons, sponges, soap
  balls of plasticene clay or foil
  fruits and vegetables like apples, tomatoes, green pepper, and onion
  pieces of cardboard, wood, blocks, Styrofoam trays, egg cartons
  grass, leaves, shells
- a dishpan or other plastic container (clear plastic is preferred)

Note: The following are not recommended for children under age two unless closely supervised by a parent:
- bottle caps (plastic and metal)
- small rocks, twigs

Activity

Fill the container with 3 to 4 inches of water. Ask your child to choose several objects. Talk to her about why she chose these objects and what may happen to them when they are put in water. Try it out. Introduce the words *float* and *sink* to describe what is happening.

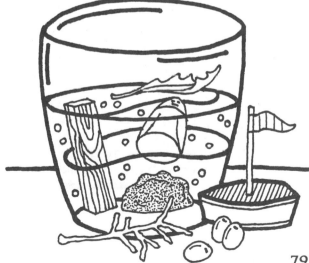

With children ages three and up who have experimented with floating and sinking before, ask them to start the activity by sorting the collection of objects. She can sort the items into piles of things that she thinks will sink and things that she thinks will float. What criteria is she using to predict the outcome?

Experiment and test her predictions. Sort the tested materials into piles of "floaters" and "sinkers." Were the before and after piles the same? Which objects behaved differently than expected?

Try placing a "sinker" on another object that will support it and allow it to float. Can all sinkers float when they are placed on a floating support?

What Your Child Is Learning

"Floating and Sinking" is a simple scientific experiment that your child is conducting, complete with making predictions, gathering evidence, and tabulating results. This activity also introduces your child to new vocabulary, words like *sink* and *float* and *heavy* and *light*.

More Things to Do

Ages three and up: Try a challenge together! Make different shapes out of plasticene clay. Can you make a shape that will float?

▶ *Be a good teacher!*

Grown-ups sometimes forget to allow for the time it takes a child to make connections between concepts. A good teacher asks a lot of questions but is always careful to allow enough time for children to think about their answers.

Fun in Winter: Snow Pictures

▶ AGES:
2 to 4+ years

▶ ACTIVITY TIME:
5 to 15 minutes

Materials

- empty, clean squeeze bottle from household cleaners (with the trigger handle), or a plant mister (Plan for between one to three colors; you will need one bottle for each color.)
- one package of food coloring
- water
- snow

Activity

Squeeze some drops of food coloring into one of the squeeze bottles. Food colors can be combined to make other colors. For example, red and yellow will make orange.

Start with about fifteen to twenty drops of color. If the color is not strong enough, you can always add more food coloring to it. Fill one third of the bottle with water and shake. Repeat the process with each color that you plan to use. For your first time trying this activity, one or two colors should be enough to keep your child interested.

Outside in the snow, find a spot where your child can use the spray bottle comfortably. Align your child so that the wind will carry the spray away from both of you. Show him how to work the spray bottle by squeezing the handle. Some spray bottles have a control on the nozzle that will adjust the type of spray from a fine mist to a directed stream.

The blanket of snow is like a big piece of paper. Encourage him to move around, using his body to make a large design rather than staying in one place. Think of this project as an outdoor painting. What kinds of lines can he make outside in the snow?

What Your Child Is Learning

This activity is something that you do just for the sheer fun of it, but it also encourages creative thinking with its unusual use of materials. The colored water looks bright against a snowy white background. In the winter, parents and children are often cooped up indoors for long periods of time. It is nice to think of a project that allows parents and children to get outside and enjoy some fresh air.

More Things to Do

Can you help him write his name in the snow?

Make a snow angel. Ask your child to lie down in the snow, with his arms at his sides. Now ask him to move his arms up above his head and back down until the snow underneath his arms is packed down. Next, he makes the same sort of movements with his feet, moving them apart to the side and then back together. To preserve the "angel" he made, he must get up carefully, without stepping in the pattern he made in the snow.

Playing with Sand

▶ AGES:
18 months to 4+ years

▶ ACTIVITY TIME:
15 to 30 minutes

Materials

- a large, flat container for sand, such as a kitty litter box, a disposable aluminum roasting pan with handles, a disposable pan for draining car oil, or a commercial sand table
- 5 to 10 pounds of washed "play sand," which is sold in toy stores and larger hardware stores
- some sand toys such as pails, shovels, scoops, sieves, funnels, sand molds, plastic cups, margarine tubs, yogurt containers, plastic toys, cars, dump trucks, other trucks, toy animals, sticks, stones, pine cones, etc.
- watering cans or empty liquid soap containers to use for adding water to the sand at a controlled rate
- for sand play outside or inside: an old plastic tarp or tablecloth for use as a ground or floor covering*

*When your child has finished playing, the tarp can be used to collect all of the sand so that it can be poured into a container and used again.

83 ◀

Activity

Fill the container with about 3 inches of sand. Sprinkle the sand lightly with water if it's dusty.

Select only a few toys and place them in the sand. Too many toys at one time can make it difficult for your child to play. Dig, mound, sift, pour, or draw in the sand. Use the sand dry or wet; explore the possibilities of both states.

To make wet sand, add water slowly until it is wet but not runny. Wet sand is great for building! Make a drip castle! In a small bowl, add water to some sand until it's runny. Take a small handful of sand and pinch your fingers together. Let the sand drip from your hand so that it forms a pile in the pan. As the sand drips, layer new sand on top of the pile.

When you are finished, leave the pan out to air-dry. When completely dry, store sand in coffee cans or other containers with tight-fitting lids.

What Your Child Is Learning

Playing with sand is a tactile experience that helps your child develop his sense of touch. Sand has some unique properties: it acts like a liquid when it is dry and like a solid when it is wet. Practice scooping, pouring, and patting down sand to exercise the imagination and refine motor skills.

More Things to Do

Color some sand! Add 3 to 4 tablespoons of powdered tempera* paint to 1 cup of sand. Stir. Store in a coffee can or tightly covered container.

Make a sand painting! See instructions for "Summer Sand Painting," p. 122.

For a wonderful related activity that you can do indoors, try "Playing with Rice" (below) for ages twelve months to four years and up.

Playing with Rice

Materials

- plastic measuring cups and measuring spoons or scoops
- 5 to 10 pounds of uncooked rice

*Powdered tempera is available at art and educational supply stores.

- a clean kitty litter box or dishpan
- **any of the following:**
    toys such as trucks, cars, or animals
    several plastic cups or containers of different sizes for filling or pouring from a funnel
- a plastic tablecloth or tarp to use as a floor covering

Activity

Lay down the floor covering and place the large container on top of it. Pour the rice into the container. Allow your child to experiment with the rice by scooping, filling, pouring, and burying. Use only a few toys at a time so that your child will have room to play.

Your child may enjoy filling up a cup with rice and pouring it back out. This can be an absorbing activity in itself. To help contain the rice, use two pans—one for scooping the rice and the other for pouring.

Use a funnel to fill a container. Funneling rice is a very different experience than funneling water.

Playspace generally agrees with the philosophy that food should not be used as a play tool. However, we've found that rice is a wonderful tactile experience for young children. It's easy to clean up, nontoxic, and inexpensive.

What Your Child Is Learning

Rice just feels good to handle. It awakens your child's sense of touch. Rice play also exercises the small muscle control needed for scooping, filling, and pouring. Scooping and pouring teach your child the meanings of words like *empty, full, big,* and *small.* This vocabulary is an essential step in his learning process, forming the foundation for understanding size and shape relationships and basic measuring.

Even More Things to Do

Provide children ages two and up with a sensory experience! Use three separate containers, each with a different material; for example, kidney beans, elbow macaroni, and rice. Fill containers with 1 to 2 inches of each material. Use with toys recommended for rice play.

Ages two and a half and up: Make sensory cards! You'll need small squares of cardboard, scissors, glue, and scraps of materials with different textures, such as sandpaper, Mylar, cotton fleece, cork, and velvet. Cut out pieces of the textured materials and glue them to the cardboard.

Play a game with your child. Put the cards in a bag. Have him reach in and pick one. Talk about what the card feels like. How many words can the two of you think of to describe the texture? When he is familiar with all of the cards, see if he can tell you which one he has chosen without removing it from the bag.

▶ *"I know that I should ask my child questions to get her to think. Where do I start?"*

Asking descriptive questions does help your child to think about what she is experiencing and learn to express herself verbally. Try to avoid questions with yes or no answers. Instead, use phrases like "why do you think" or "what would happen if" or "how did you" to involve your child in the activity. Instead of asking, "Can you pour the sand?" ask, "What would happen if you poured the sand from the big container into that little cup?" "Why do you think it didn't all fit?" "Is there anything else we could use to pour sand into that is the right size?"

▶ *"Is my child too young for this activity? I am afraid that he may eat the sand or the rice."*

It is natural for your child to behave like this. All young children will experiment by eating things that they shouldn't from time to time. Go ahead and play. Sand and uncooked rice are nontoxic and will not harm your child.

Over, Under, Around, and Through: An Obstacle Course Built Just for You

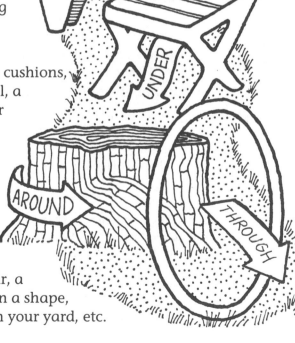

▶ **AGES:**
18 months to 4+ years

▶ **ACTIVITY TIME:**
5 to 25 minutes

Materials

♦ a combination of any of the following items that your child could move around safely:

To climb over: lawn chair or foam cushions, a child-sized chair, a big beach ball, a low plastic outdoor table, Mom's or Dad's lap while they are sitting on the ground, etc.

To climb under: a picnic table, an adult-sized chair, a lawn chair, a big bush, an empty baby pool, a length of clothesline held by two people, trees, etc.

To go around: a hula hoop, a chair, a length of rope laid on the ground in a shape, a tree or other natural landmark in your yard, etc.

To go through: a cardboard appliance box with the flaps removed from both ends, a hula hoop, two lightweight chairs propped together to make a tunnel, Mom or Dad on their hands and knees in the yard, etc.

Activity

Select a spot for your obstacle course where the ground is flat and open. The rest is simple. For younger children, set up one or two things at first. Start with an object like a hula hoop. Can your child walk around the hula hoop? Is she familiar with the word *around?* Can she change directions? Can she hop into the center? Add another "obstacle." Walk your child through the course that you have set up. As you both try out each obstacle, introduce her to the new vocabulary words.

With older children two years and up, you can make the obstacle course more complicated and challenging. Choose from some of the suggested items above to create your course, or use your own imagination to make use of your child's toys and household objects. Set up a different area for each word—*over, under, around,* and *through.* Once she has mastered the course, you can time her with your watch to see how fast she is able to complete certain parts of the course. Can she go through the course backward? With one hand behind her back?

Sit back, relax, and watch your child practice her motor skills—that is, unless you are one of the "obstacles" in the course.

What Your Child Is Learning

When your child is active and moving she is practicing gross motor skills and coordination. This activity combines healthy exercise with some new vocabulary words in a refreshingly different way.

> ▶ Children learn best by doing. Use a hula hoop to teach your child the meaning of the four words *over, under, around,* and *through.* Show her how to step *over* the hoop and walk *around* the hoop while it is lying on the ground, climb *under* the hoop while you hold it in the air, and step *through* the hoop while you hold it next to your side.

More Things to Do

Try this activity with a group of kids. With a group of three- and four-year-olds, you can ask the children to be the "obstacles" instead of furniture or toys. Take turns having children go through the course.

For young children, use a hand puppet to act out the words *over, under, around,* and *through.*

After you are through with your obstacle course, have a tall glass of lemonade.

Wind Costumes

▶ **AGES:**
2 to 4+ years

▶ **ACTIVITY TIME:**
**10 to 15 minutes
to make**

Materials

♦ a piece of lightweight cardboard or tagboard big enough to wrap loosely around your child's wrist (one piece for each bracelet)
♦ any of the following materials to make streamers: tissue paper, ribbons, crepe paper, Mylar, plastic lawn bags, newspaper
♦ scissors
♦ tape

Activity

Precut the cardboard into strips 2 inches thick. Make sure that the board fits your child's wrist loosely, with about 2 inches of overlap.

Precut the streamer material(s) into strips between 6 and 12 inches long and ½ to 1 inch thick. Streamers can be all different lengths.

(1) CUT CARDBOARD STRIPS

2"

(2) CHECK FIT

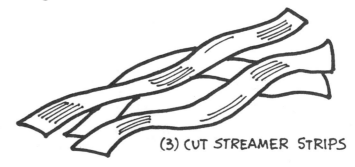

(3) CUT STREAMER STRIPS

Invite your child to select some of the streamers and tape them onto the board. The streamers should go all the way from one end of the strip to the other.

When your child is finished, fit the bracelet around her wrist so that it is comfortable. To make an interlocking clasp for the bracelet, place two cuts about $1\frac{1}{2}$ inches from the edge of the board. The cuts should be on opposite ends on each side, so that the bracelet can interlock when it wraps around (see illustration).

(4) TAPE STREAMERS AND CUT INTERLOCKING CLASPS

Go outside and enjoy the wind! What happens to streamers in windy spots? Compare open spaces to places where there is little wind. Run and move with the streamers; make your own wind!

What Your Child Is Learning

She is learning about wind, air currents, and how wind moves. She is looking for signs of the wind. Wearing the streamers makes her more aware of her body, inviting her to explore motion and self-expression through movement.

More Things to Do

Look for other evidence of wind when you are out walking. Listen for leaves rustling, look for branches swaying, flags flapping, or smoke rising from chimneys.

Make wind anklets to match the wind bracelets.

Night-Light

► AGES:
2 to 4+ years

► ACTIVITY TIME:
15 to 25 minutes
to make

Materials

- a clear plastic soda bottle (1 or 2 liter), rinsed, clean and dry, and with the label removed. Remove the cap and save it.
- multicolored tissue paper, in light colors (so that the light will shine through) cut into relatively large pieces, about 2 by 2 inches
- white glue thinned with water: three parts glue to one part water
- a container for glue
- a brush*
- a craft knife
- a powerful flashlight, small enough to fit a soda bottle
- duct tape
- scissors
- a piece of string or yarn 12 inches long
- lots of newspaper or a tarp to cover the work surface. This is a messy project.

*To make your own paste and paint brush, see "How to Make a Paste and Paint Brush," p. 210.

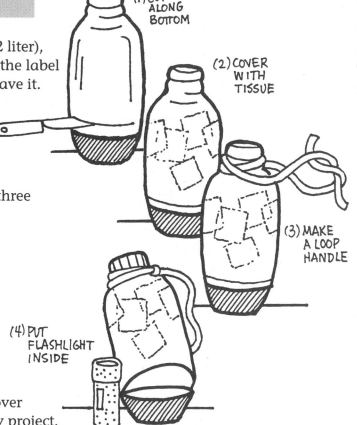

(1) CUT ALONG BOTTOM

(2) COVER WITH TISSUE

(3) MAKE A LOOP HANDLE

(4) PUT FLASHLIGHT INSIDE

Activity	This project has two steps that should be completed before you begin working with your child. First, with a craft knife, cut a line three quarters of the way around the bottom of the soda bottle. If your soda bottle has a piece of plastic attached to the bottom, cut above the point where the plastic meets the clear soda bottle. Do not remove the bottom of the bottle completely. This is where you will insert the flashlight when the lantern is completed.

Next, cut the tissue paper into any shapes you like. Make some 2-inch squares because they cover the surface area of the bottle the most efficiently. Now you are ready to work with your child.

Prepare the work surface. Place the soda bottle, tissue shapes, glue, and the glue brush on the table within easy reach of your child. He may begin by choosing a piece of tissue. With a younger child, ask him to hold the tissue where he likes on the carton while you brush over it with the glue. Older children can handle the whole task on their own.

Cover as much of the soda bottle as you can using the tissue and glue mixture. Layering colors gives an interesting effect. Allow the lantern to dry thoroughly.

(5) SECURE WITH DUCT TAPE

To Make a Handle
When the lantern is dry, loop the piece of string around the grooves on the bottle neck where the cap fits. Wrap the string so that it makes one full turn around the bottle neck. Take the bottle cap that you put aside, and screw it down tightly onto the soda bottle. Tie the ends of the pieces of string together to form a loop. This loop will become your handle.

To Add Light
Bend back the flap in the bottom of the soda bottle. Turn on your flashlight. Place the flashlight inside the bottom of the soda bottle, so that the light is facing up. Fold back the flap and secure the bottom with pieces of duct tape.

With Your Finished Lantern

Let your child lead you on an early evening walk. Things look different in light from a lantern. Everything seems more mysterious. Explore the corners of your yard. Make the light dance. Throw shadows. Explore the different movements you can make with your arms.

Note: If you would like to ensure the longevity of your lantern, you can seal the tissue with a protective spray. See the instructions for using sealants in the "Bird Feeder" activity, p. 67.

What Your Child Is Learning

Your child is learning that light creates shadows and illuminates all that is around it. He is learning that when you put colors in front of a light, the light will take on the cast of the different hues. Colored lanterns have a festive feel to them. You can use this project to celebrate a special occasion or to help your child get over his fear of the dark.

More Things to Do

Find your shadow on a sunny day.

Get some friends together and have a lantern-making party. Plan an evening walk for when the lanterns are dry.

If you have a cat, try this game. In the evening, turn out the lights in a room of your house and see if your cat will chase a flashlight beam.

> ▶ In the Jamaica Plain neighborhood of Boston, every fall there is a lantern walk around Jamaica Pond for families in the community. The walk takes place at dusk. It is a beautiful sight to see the bobbing lights of all the walkers strung out around the length of the pond.

CHAPTER 4
Seasonal Activities

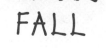

Printing with Fall Leaves

▶ **AGES:**
18 months to 4+ years

▶ **ACTIVITY TIME:**
10 to 25 minutes

Materials

- an assortment of leaves of different shapes and sizes
- tempera paint, either powdered or premixed (available at art supply, craft and hobby, and educational supply stores)
- paintbrushes, preferably one for each color*
- construction paper or other heavy paper at least 8½ by 11 inches
- newspaper, plastic tray, or place mat to print on
- extra newspaper to print on and for drying finished work
- a paint container** or Styrofoam tray
- a smock or old adult-sized shirt for your child to wear (optional)

*See instructions for "How to Make a Paste and Paint Brush," p. 210.
**See "How to Make a 'No-Spill' Paint Container," p. 211.

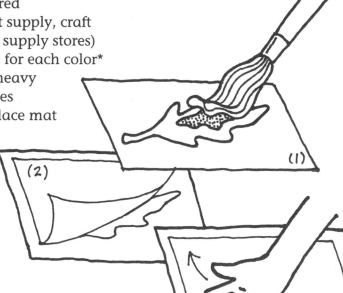

Activity	Pour a small amount of paint into a paint container or Styrofoam tray. Choose a leaf to print. Lay the leaf on a piece of newspaper. With the brush, coat the leaf with a thin layer of paint. Gently lift the leaf by the stem and place it on a clean piece of newspaper. Lay your child's paper over it and ask him to rub the paper with the palm of his hand. Repeat the process with different shapes and colors of leaves.

Another technique is to fold a piece of paper in half. After you and your child paint the leaf, slip the leaf inside the paper fold. Help your child to smooth over the paper evenly with his hand.

This project requires only one color of paint, but for best results, two or three colors are recommended. Fall colors like yellow, orange, and red are especially vibrant when paired with a deep purple or blue. Also, switch paper colors. Lighter shades will show the leaves most clearly. |
| **What Your Child Is Learning** | Your child is observing leaves, learning about the seasons and what happens to trees in the fall. He also learns that leaves have stems and veins. This project teaches appreciation of and respect for the natural world. It also encourages attention to detail. |
| **More Things to Do** | Collect more leaves and other natural things and make a collage using clear contact paper. Individual leaves laminated between two pieces of clear contact paper can be turned into fall decorations. Trim excess with scissors and tape to a window. |

▶ LEAVES

Red and yellow, gold and brown
See the leaves come floating down

Cut some leaf shapes out of colored construction paper. Holding the leaves in your hand, stand on a chair. While reciting the poem, open your hands and let the leaves fall to the ground. Ask your child to catch the leaves as they fall.

Design a fall tree! You'll need a piece of heavy paper, construction or tissue paper in fall colors, a crayon, paste, and a brush. Draw a tree trunk on a piece of heavy paper. The trunk should take up no more than half of the height of the paper. The rest of the paper should be left blank. Tear or cut the colored paper into rounded shapes to resemble leaves. Together, you and your child can paste the leaves in the blank space left on the paper.

Make a crayon rubbing with fall leaves. See "Creative Crayon Rubbings," p. 131.

In the Apple Tree

Tune: a chant, a rap, or a song of your own

Song and Movements

Way up high in the apple tree (arms stretched high)
Two little apples smiled at me (Make a circle with your thumb and pointer finger)

I shook that tree as hard as I could (shake out your arms)
Down came the apples (bring your arms down)
Ummm, they were good (rub your tummy)
(Repeat quickly)

What Your Child Is Learning

This song uses pretend play and arm motions to pantomime apple picking. Your child is learning a seasonal song and experiencing the concepts of high and low.

Halloween Pumpkin Wands

▶ **AGES:**
18 months to 4+ years

▶ **ACTIVITY TIME:**
5 to 20 minutes

Materials

- ◆ a paper plate
- ◆ scissors and a pencil
- ◆ a Popsicle (craft) stick
- ◆ masking tape
- ◆ orange tempera paint, either powdered or premixed (available at art supply, craft and hobby, and educational supply stores)
- ◆ a piece of brown construction paper or a brown marker or crayon for the stem
- ◆ a piece of black construction paper
- ◆ newspaper, plastic tray, or place mat to paint on
- ◆ a smock or old adult-sized shirt for your child to wear (optional)

CUT ALONG OUTLINE SHAPE

Activity	First, outline the shape of a pumpkin on the paper plate. A pumpkin is shaped like a heart, but with a flat bottom instead of a point. Include a wedge shape for the stem. The tracing should be almost as large as the plate. Cut out the pumpkin shape with scissors.
	Secure the Popsicle stick to the back of the plate with masking tape. Next, precut the black construction paper into jack-o'-lantern shapes. Cut out triangles for eyes or the nose, a mouth with teeth, or any shapes you wish. Precut a stem out of brown paper. If you don't have brown paper, use a marker to color a piece of white paper.
	Brush a thin layer of orange paint on a Styrofoam tray or pie tin. Present the paint, the brush, and the pumpkin to your child. He can cover the paper plate with orange paint. Use the wet paint to affix the eyes, nose and mouth, and stem.
What Your Child Is Learning	Making a pumpkin wand is a fun way to get into the holiday spirit. Halloween is a magical time for young children because they still believe in fantasy. Making a pumpkin wand with its own personality encourages imagination and pretend play.
More Things to Do	Make a trick-or-treat bag! You need a paper shopping bag with handles, white tempera paint, orange and black paper cut into shapes, and glue. Cover the shopping bag with two coats of white paint to cover any writing or logo. When the paint dries, your child can collage the Halloween picture onto the bag. Allow the bag to sit overnight before using.
	Be a pumpkin scientist! Cut open a pumpkin and compare the inside to the outside. Look at the meat, the seeds, the skin, and the stem.

I'm a Little Pumpkin

Tune: "I'm a Little Teapot"

Song

I'm a little pumpkin
Oh so round
I grow on a vine
Very close to the ground

Halloween is coming
What shall I do?
I need a face
To look at you

I'm a little pumpkin
Oh so round
I grow on a vine
Very close to the ground

Halloween is coming
I know what to do
I have a face
To smile at you

Activity

Make a pumpkin wand, carve a
pumpkin, or draw a pumpkin face.

 102

Making Holiday Ornaments

▶ **AGES:**
    18 months to 4+ years

▶ **ACTIVITY TIME:**
    15 to 35 minutes

Materials

- ◆ cardboard, poster board, or tagboard to cut into simple shapes
- ◆ things to decorate with, such as colored tissue paper, shiny paper, fabric or felt scraps, tempera paint, and a paint tray
- ◆ scissors
- ◆ a craft knife or cut cardboard (optional)
- ◆ paste or glue and a brush*
- ◆ yarn or string
- ◆ a hole punch or scissors
- ◆ brass paper fasteners for attaching pieces (optional)
- ◆ glitter (optional—only for children over three)
- ◆ newspaper to cover the work surface
- ◆ a smock or old adult-sized shirt for your child to wear (optional)

Note: Glitter is hazardous for young children who might accidentally eat or inhale the metal particles. Use glitter only with children three years and over, and take care to supervise your child when using it.

*See instructions for "How to Make a Paste and Paint Brush," p. 210.

| Activity | Ahead of time, cut the cardboard or tagboard into holiday shapes large enough for your child to decorate. If you use brass paper fasteners and thin board, you can make two shapes and join them together to create movable ornaments. |

Ahead of time, cut the cardboard or tagboard into holiday shapes large enough for your child to decorate. If you use brass paper fasteners and thin board, you can make two shapes and join them together to create movable ornaments.

With brown cardboard, before you start, cover the basic shape with a piece of colored paper or a coat of paint. This way the cardboard won't show on the finished ornament.

Next, arrange the decorating materials and paste on the table along with one cardboard shape. Encourage your child to choose materials that catch his eye. Attach them with paste. Paper materials will adhere to tempera paint. Usually, paint can be substituted for paste for a different look. Ages three and up may choose to use glitter with wet glue or paint with help from a parent.

When dry, punch a hole in the top of the ornament. Loop a piece of string through the hole. Your ornament is ready to hang.

What Your Child Is Learning

Making ornaments is one way in which your child can participate in the preparations for holiday celebrations that are important to you. In this way, he begins to learn about the beliefs and sentiment that are part of the meaning of family holidays. His contribution to your family traditions, no matter how small, demonstrates to him that he has a place in your family.

More Things to Do

Children three and up: Make papier-mâché ornaments. For papier-mâché you will need: newspaper torn into strips; a cardboard or Styrofoam shape; flour; water; a small plastic bowl and a brush and paint for the finished ornament.

Tear newspaper into half-inch-wide strips of different lengths. Combine 2 tablespoons of flour with 4 tablespoons of water to make paste. Stir. Dip a strip of news-

paper into the paste mixture. Wipe off the excess paste with your fingers. Lay the strip over the cardboard or foam shape. Paste overlapping strips, first going one direction, then another. Cover the shape with at least three layers of paper. Don't forget to papier-mâché the back of your ornament. Paint finished projects with tempera paint, once they have dried thoroughly.

Make a holiday snack or teach your child a holiday song to sing!

▶ Wallpaper paste makes a terrific glue for papier-mâché. Look for small packages marked "cellulose" at the hardware store. Water is added to the dry mixture to make a strong, nontoxic glue that does not feel sticky on your hands.

I'm a Little Snowman

Tune: "I'm a Little Teapot"

Song and Movements

I'm a little snowman	(arms circle above your head)
Round and fat	(arms circle down)
Here are my buttons	(point to buttons down chest)
Here is my hat	(point to head)
I have two eyes, a mouth	(point to eyes and mouth)
And a carrot nose	(point to nose)
And a scarf to keep me warm	
when the cold wind blows	(point to neck)

What Your Child Is Learning

This seasonal song uses listening skills to cue the corresponding hand motions. The hand motions teach her to identify parts of the body and reinforce her understanding of body awareness.

Snowy Night Paintings

► **AGES:**
18 months to 4+ years

► **ACTIVITY TIME:**
10 to 20 minutes

Materials

- black construction paper, at least 8½ by 11 inches
- white tempera paint, either powdered or premixed
- a paintbrush*
- a paint container or Styrofoam tray
- newspaper, plastic try, or place mat to paint on
- cotton balls, quilting, or pillow stuffing
- white glue and a glue brush*
- glitter (optional—only for children three and over)
- a smock or old adult-sized shirt for your child to wear (optional)

*To make your own brush, see "How to Make a Paste and Paint Brush," p. 210.

Activity

Place the paint and brush within easy reach of the child. She can use the brush freely. Sweeping lines look like snow-covered trees and dots look like big flakes of snow.

After her painting dries, add wisps of snow with cotton balls or pillow stuffing. Cotton balls can be pulled apart to form tufts. Tack the materials on with white glue.

Children three and up may add glitter to their paintings. Glitter should be used sparingly over a large piece of scrap paper for a quick cleanup.

What Your Child Is Learning

The project asks your child to think about phenomena she has experienced, like nighttime and possibly snow. What is it like at night? What does she do in the dark? What does snow feel like? Painting a nighttime picture should stimulate conversation and curiosity in your child about her surroundings. For very young children painting is good practice for hand-eye coordination; it exercises their muscles and their imaginations.

▶ ICE SKATING

(Tune: a chant, a rap, or a song of your own)

Ice skating is nice skating
Everyone loves to go ice skating
Sliding around and turning so
One, two, three, and away we go
Ice skating is nice skating
Everyone loves to go ice skating

More Things to Do

Make hand prints with white paint on black paper. See "Hand Prints," p. 27.

What about a winter collage? Use white or black paper, cotton balls or pillow stuffing, shiny paper, and paste. For fun, cut the paper into the shape of a snowflake before your child begins her collage. Hang your finished snowflake from a string.

Read your child a nighttime or snowy story, such as *In the Night Kitchen* by Maurice Sendak or *A Snowy Day,* by Ezra Jack Keats.

▶ SNOWFLAKES

(Tune: a chant, a rap, or a song of your own)

Snowflakes falling all around
Falling gently to the ground
Snowflakes make the world so grand
Like a winter wonderland

Special-Occasion Cards

▶ AGES:	▶ ACTIVITY TIME:
18 months to 4+ years	*15 to 35 minutes*

Materials

- construction paper, heavy paper, tagboard, or card stock (card stock is available at art supply and stationery stores)
- any of the following:
  paste, glue, and a brush or glue sticks (for *over age three*) to use with papers cut into shapes: construction paper, colored tissues, shiny paper, or wrapping paper scraps
  markers, crayons, or oil pastels
  rubber stamps and a stamp pad, string blocks or sponge stamps
- newspaper to cover the work surface
- a smock or old adult-sized shirt for your child to wear (optional)

Activity

Cut and fold your paper to size. A 5- by 7-inch card will fit into a standard card envelope. For a card that flips open, start with a piece of paper 10 by 7 inches and fold it in half in the middle. Tagboard makes nice postcard-style cards.

Rubber stamps and other printing methods are suggested when you are planning to make multiple cards, because they are relatively fast to make. For ideas about how to use stamps and other materials, you may want to refer to "How to Make Easy Potato Stamps" (p. 217), and "Printing with Fruits and Vegetables" (p. 42).

Lay out the materials that will be used for the card. Help your child to decide how she will decorate the card. Maybe it is for her grandmother, whose favorite color is blue. Discuss with your child who the card is for, what the occasion is, and what she would like to say.

What Your Child Is Learning

Your child is learning that cards are one way to let someone special know that you care about them. Your child is learning to communicate with words. Helping your child make her own card is a way to help her to articulate her feelings. Help her formulate what she would like to say. This is a constructive way to reinforce talking about both positive and negative emotions.

More Things to Do

Make "Beautiful Dyed Paper" (see p. 46). Cut pieces that fit a 5- by 7-inch format. Cutting paper to $4\frac{1}{2}$ by $6\frac{1}{2}$ inches will create a border. Glue paper to the card.

See instructions for "Sponge Printing" (p.40) or "Printing with String" (p.44).

Valentine Hearts

► AGES:
18 months to 4+ years

► ACTIVITY TIME:
10 to 20 minutes

Materials

- red construction paper 8½ by 11 inches or 12 by 18 inches
- pink and white tempera paint, either powdered or premixed (available at art supply, craft and hobby, and educational supply stores)
- paintbrushes, one for each color if possible
- pink and white tissue cut into 1-inch-thick streamers
- silver and gold paper, like wrapping paper or Mylar, cut into small pieces
- doilies cut into wedge shapes
- newspaper, plastic tray, or place mat to paint on
- a smock or old adult-sized shirt for your child to wear (optional)

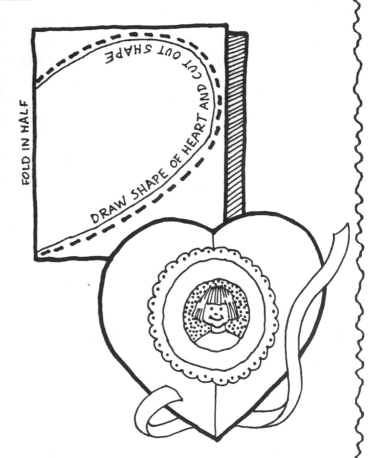

FOLD IN HALF

DRAW SHAPE OF HEART AND CUT OUT SHAPE

| **Activity** | First, cut the construction paper into the shape of a heart. Set out the paint and decorating materials. Invite your child to paint on the heart shape. Together, attach collage pieces to the heart, using the paint like glue. Decorate the outline of the heart with tissue streamers. |

| **What Your Child Is Learning** | This activity gives young children the pleasure of giving a homemade gift to someone special. Sharing a card he made with someone teaches your child about sentiment. He is learning to communicate his feelings through positive actions. |

| **More Things to Do** | Sponge-print a Valentine's Day card. See "Sponge Printing," p. 40. |

Personalize your valentine! Design a valentine heart. Paste a doilie in the middle. Cut a photo of your child into the shape of a circle and paste it in the center.

WILL YOU BE MY VALENTINE?

(Tune: "London Bridge Is Falling Down")

Will you be my valentine
Valentine, valentine
Will you be my valentine
My very special friend

I will be your valentine
Valentine, valentine
I will be your valentine
My very special friend

Collage of Spring Flowers

▶ **AGES:**
12 months to 4+ years

▶ **ACTIVITY TIME:**
5 to 15 minutes

Materials

- construction paper, at least 8½ by 11 inches, in spring colors
- colored tissue (optional)
- scissors
- paste or glue and a brush*
- a real tulip, daffodil, or crocus or pictures of flowers for your child to identify (optional)
- newspaper, plastic place mat, or tray for pasting
- a wet cloth for cleanup

Activity

Ahead of time, cut construction paper or colored tissue paper into flower shapes. Cut pieces for petals, flower centers, stems, and leaves. Triangular shapes are good for tulips; ruffled shapes make fine daffodils; thin, spiky

*See "How to Make a Paste or Paint Brush," p. 210.

▶ 114

shapes look like crocus leaves. Use your imagination to invent your own spring flowers. Arrange the flower pieces on the worktable.

Ask your child to choose a piece of construction paper for the background. Look at the flower shapes you made and at the flowers or photographs if you have them. If she likes, draw a line on the paper or cut strips of construction paper to indicate the ground.

Look at some real flowers or pictures. Talk to her about the parts of a flower and how they grow. Help your child construct flowers on the background paper from the parts you prepared. Stick the pieces down with paste and a brush. Use a wet cloth to wipe sticky fingers.

What Your Child Is Learning

This project helps your child identify spring flowers and learn about how they grow. It is a way of celebrating spring and instilling an appreciation for nature and an interest in growing things.

More Things to Do

Plant bean seeds together! You'll need a bag of dried beans (lima or another variety), a Dixie cup, dirt, and a pencil. Soak bean seeds in water overnight. Poke a hole in the bottom of the Dixie cup with a pencil. Fill three quarters of the cup with dirt. With the pencil, poke a hole in the dirt large enough for a bean. Place a bean in the hole. Pat the soil down firmly on top of it. Water and keep in a window. Beans germinate quickly; you should have results within two weeks.

▶ LITTLE FLOWER

(Crunch up a piece of clear plastic kitchen wrap in your hand. Close it tightly).

Little flower closed up tight
Opens up to see the light

(Open your hand slowly. Keep your hand cupped so that the plastic wrap opens in the shape of a flower.)

Plant grass! Follow the instructions on page 115, but in this case sprinkle grass seed on top of the soil. Add a little bit of dirt to cover the seed. Water and place in a well-lit area. Remember to keep soil wet.

Take a walk and look for spring flowers!

▶ *Why are collage materials like a set of blocks?*

Because both collage materials and blocks grow along with your child. As your child develops, the way he approaches materials will change too. As he grows he will begin to build intricate structures and draw complicated pictures. Both blocks and art materials have unlimited potential to adapt to your child's need for challenge.

▶ For children three and a half and up we recommend: scissors; markers; pencils; crayons or colored chalk; mementos like photos, stamps, postcards; and craft store supplies like brightly colored feathers, doilies, colored cellophane, fabric and felt pieces.

Spring Song

Tune: a chant, rap, or song of your own

Materials
- any of the following: spring flowers, pictures or drawings of spring flowers for your child to identify

Song

First comes the crocus, the crocus, the crocus
First comes the crocus
Oh, yes it does

Next comes the daffodil,
the daffodil, the daffodil
Next comes the daffodil
Oh, yes it does

Then comes the tulip,
the tulip, the tulip
Then comes the tulip
Oh, yes it does

May Streamer Dance and May Streamers

Tune: "London Bridge Is Falling Down"

Materials

- ◆ colorful streamers, two for each child and adult
  (see instructions for "May Streamers" to follow)

Song and Movements

It's the merry month of May
Month of May, month of May
It's the merry month of May
Come and dance with me.

(Children dance around freely with the streamers)

Walk to the right now, one, two, three
One, two, three; one, two, three
Walk to the right now, one, two, three
Come and dance with me.

(Children walk to the right, dance freely on the last line)

Promenade left now, let me see
Let me see, let me see
Promenade left now, let me see
Come and dance with me.

(Children walk to the left, dance freely on the last line)

Shake it in and shake it out
In and out, in and out
Shake it in and shake it out
Come and dance with me.

(Shake the streamer in and out, dance freely on the last line)

Do your own dance, if you will
If you will, if you will
Do your own dance, if you will
Your very special way.

What Your Child Is Learning

This song emphasizes sequencing and following directions, while also giving your child the opportunity to express himself. Singing songs with children gives them an appreciation of language and sounds as well as a familiarity with music.

May
Streamers

Materials

- pipe cleaners
- tissue paper cut into long strips, 1 inch wide and between 14 and 18 inches long
- Mylar cut into long strips, 1 inch wide and between 14 and 18 inches long
- scissors or a hole punch

Activity

Punch or poke a hole in the end of the tissue and Mylar strips, about half an inch from the edge.

Thread the streamers onto the pipe cleaner, one at a time. When you have collected a bunch of streamers, twist the two ends of the pipe cleaner together to form a ring that your child can hold on to. Be careful to tuck in or snip off any sharp edges from the wire inside the pipe cleaner.

Chilly Icicle Paintings

Materials

- ◆ an ice cube tray
- ◆ Popsicle (craft) sticks (available from art supply, craft and hobby, and educational supply stores)
- ◆ powdered tempera paint (available where craft sticks are sold)
- ◆ empty salt or spice shakers, one for each color of paint
- ◆ newspaper, place mat, or plastic tray to paint on
- ◆ extra newspaper to cover the floor
- ◆ finger paint paper, freezer wrap paper, or heavy, shiny paper
- ◆ a smock or old adult-sized shirt for your child to wear (optional)

Activity

Prepare the ice cube "paintbrushes" the night before. Fill the ice cube tray with water and add a Popsicle stick to each compartment. It's okay if the sticks don't stand up straight.

Prepare the work surface. Place powdered tempera in the shakers. Give the child a piece of paper and an ice cube "paintbrush." Rub the ice pops across the shiny paper. Then sprinkle different colors of powdered tempera onto the paper.

The water and the powdered paint will combine to make a unique picture. He can use his paintbrush to move the powdered paint around on the paper.

What Your Child Is Learning	Your child is learning about the properties of ice. Ice is cold and hard when it comes from the freezer, but soon it melts and becomes water. As water, ice can combine easily with other materials, like powdered paint.
More Things to Do	Make juice pops! Fill the compartments in the ice cube trays with your favorite kind of fruit juice. Insert a Popsicle stick in each compartment and freeze. When juice is frozen you can see a crystalline pattern.

Summer Sand Painting

Materials

- ◆ a bag of children's play sand from a toy or hardware store
- ◆ construction paper or other heavy paper about 8½ by 11 inches
- ◆ white glue, preferably in a small glue bottle with a twist cap
- ◆ a Popsicle (craft) stick (to use with glue if you do not have a squeeze bottle)
- ◆ Dixie cups
- ◆ newspaper, plastic place mat, or tray for gluing
- ◆ a dishpan or shallow plastic tub (paper should lie flat on the bottom)

To Color the Sand (optional)
- ◆ dry tempera paints
- ◆ a cookie sheet or pie tin, one for each color
- ◆ waxed paper
- ◆ a spoon
- ◆ measuring cup
- ◆ plastic containers or coffee cans with lids for storage

Activity

This project can be done with sand right out of the bag, or with colored sand. Colored sand can be made ahead of time and stored in a coffee can.

To Color the Sand
Mix 3 to 4 teaspoons of dry tempera for 1 cup of dry sand. Stir with a spoon. Store sand in a coffee can or tightly covered container.

To Make a Sand Painting

Pour a little bit of sand into a Dixie cup. Set it aside. If you do not have a squeeze bottle of glue, pour a little glue into a Dixie cup so that the bottom of the cup is covered with a thin layer of glue. Dip a craft stick into the glue and show your child how to "draw" with the stick. Colored paper makes the glue easy to see.

Place the paper in the bottom of the plastic tub. Give your child the cup of sand. Help him shake the sand onto the picture, covering the glue design. Carefully lift up the picture and shake it over the tub to remove excess sand.

You can add more glue to the picture and then more sand. With colored sand, add a different color of sand each time to make a multicolored picture.

Note: A small bottle of white glue with a cap is convenient because it's easier to control how much glue gets on the paper.

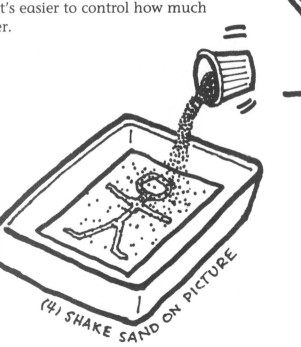

(2) COFFEE CAN TO DIXIE CUP

(3) PAINT WITH GLUE

GLUE

(4) SHAKE SAND ON PICTURE

123 ◀

What Your Child Is Learning

Playing with sand is a tactile experience for young children, because of its grainy texture and the way it slips through their fingers. Making a sand painting gives your child the opportunity to experience a natural material with unique properties.

More Things to Do

Sift and pour! See "Playing with Sand," p. 83.

With older children, look at the sand under a magnifying glass. What do you see?

Compare wet and dry sand. You'll need two medium-sized plastic bowls and a plastic tarp to play with the sand on. Fill one third of each bowl with sand. Add a little bit of water to one bowl and leave the other bowl dry. Place the sand from each bowl on opposite sides of the plastic. Use your fingers and different tools such as spoons, toy cars, and small plastic containers to explore the differences in how the sand behaves.

▶ *Are you looking for an unusual gift idea?*

Colored sand can be layered in a glass jar with a lid for an interesting present.

Summer Song

Tune: "Skip to My Lou"

Song

Chorus
Summer is my favorite time
Summer is my favorite time
Summer is my favorite time
My favorite time of year

Let's go swimming at the beach
Let's go swimming in the lake
Let's go swimming at the pool
Just to keep us cool

(Chorus)

Picnics are a lot of fun
Picnics are for everyone
Playing Frisbee on the run
Underneath the sun

(Chorus)

What Your Child Is Learning

This song is a celebration of summer and warm-weather activities.

CHAPTER 5
Quiet Activities

Drawing with Your Child

Materials

- paper or scrap paper. For younger toddlers, paper should be at least 8½ by 11 inches
- tape
- any of the following: water-soluble, washable markers; colored chalk; chunk-style crayons*; "jumbo" crayons; "anti-roll" crayons (they have one flat side); or "jumbo" oil pastels. All of these are available at educational and art supply stores.

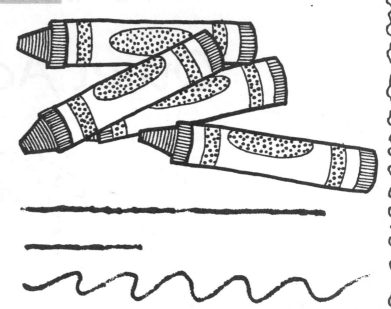

Activity

Provide your child with paper and drawing materials. Tape a piece of paper to a flat surface. For younger toddlers who are just learning to make lines, markers are suggested. Markers are easier for young children to use because they do not require too much hand pressure. When using markers, limit the child to one marker at a time to control accidental coloring.

If you don't like to use markers or your child is still mouthing things, crayons are

*To make your own chunk-style crayons, see "How to Make Round Crayons," p. 213.

okay. We suggest either "jumbo" or chunk-style sticks. Their large size is easy for young children to hold on to.

Children are naturally interested in drawing and usually require little more than to be shown how to hold the marker before they can experiment on their own. Drawing is a fascinating way to watch your child's development. Children begin by scribbling a few lines, then lose interest. But as they grow and develop creativity and coordination, they will progress to circles, letters, and recognizable pictures.

Help younger children to become familiar with colors. You can ask your child to "draw with the red crayon," while handing him the red crayon. With older children, you can talk about different lines or shapes. Can you make a long line? A short line? A crazy line? A dotted line? Polka dots? See how many variations you can come up with.

Make movement part of the drawing project. Take long steps around the room to suggest long lines, then short steps for short lines. Hop to make a dotted line. Ask your child to lead you on a zigzag line. Put on some music if you like. Make a drawing that expresses the feeling of the music using lines and colors.

Many parents are unsure of how to talk about their child's drawings. Asking, "Is it a horse?" or, "What is it?" can limit your child's imagination by asking him to conform to an adult's idea of what a picture should be. His drawing may not be a "thing." Instead, ask your child, "Tell me about your picture." This enables your child to formulate his own ideas.

Similarly, a parent will often praise a child with "Your picture is beautiful." A more meaningful approach would be to compliment a specific part of the picture. Look for a part of the drawing where the lines, colors, or shapes are interesting to you. "I like how the blue line looks next to the red circle." Mentioning a specific element of the picture will seem more sincere and help him look at relationships between different elements in the drawing.

What Your Child Is Learning

Drawing with your child will encourage self-expression and creativity. Drawing regularly with your child can improve your child's concentration. It is also a powerful and satisfying means of expression for preschoolers who can't always say everything they want to say with words.

More Things to Do

Talk about shapes or colors with your child. Shapes can be tall or short, wide or thin, round or straight. Colors can be daytime or nighttime, happy or sad, summer or winter. What is your child's favorite color?

Trace your child's hand and let him color it in.

Draw with colored chalk on a sidewalk or driveway. You will need "jumbo" pieces of chalk (either white or multicolored) from a toy or art supply store. This is the perfect opportunity to introduce your child to a game of hopscotch. You can use a hose to clean up, or leave your pictures for a little while and let the first rain wash them away.

With older children ages three and up: Design your own drawing machine! Bunch a few different colored markers together and secure with a rubber band. Draw with all of the colors at once.

Keep a collection of your child's drawings as he grows. See "How to Make a Portfolio for Your Child's Artwork," p. 234.

Note: To clean up stray crayon marks or marker, use automotive hand cleaner and a soft rag. See "About Setting Up Activities" for more information.

> ▶ Chalk is one of our favorite drawing materials in Playspace. Draw with colored chalk on black construction paper for vivid results. Show older children how the chalk will blur if you rub over it with your finger. Fix the chalk surface on your finished picture with a touch of hair spray.

Creative Crayon Rubbings

▶ AGES:
18 months to 4+ years

▶ ACTIVITY TIME:
10 to 15 minutes

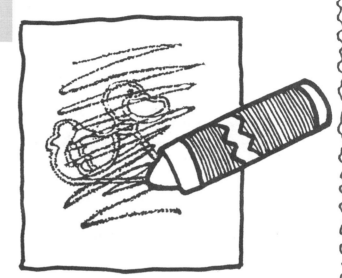

Materials

- paper
- crayons
  for children under three: jumbo size, "anti-roll" (with a flat side), and "chunk-style" crayons
  for children three and up: any of the above and standard-sized crayons
- an assortment of flat items to make rubbings from: leaves, plastic disks, shapes cut from heavy paper, sandpaper, stencils, string, etc.
- a place mat or plastic tray to use as a work surface (optional)
- tape

Activity

Place the items you are making rubbings of on a flat surface. You may choose to make a rubbing with lots of items or just one or two.

*To make your own chunk crayons, see "How to Make Round Crayons," p. 213.

Place one or two objects on the tabletop and cover the objects with a sheet of paper. Tape the paper in place. Use paper that is big enough to allow some room around the edges for coloring, so that your child will not color on the table accidentally.

To make a large rubbing, place many items underneath a large piece of paper. You can buy rolls of paper at educational, art supply, and office supply stores.

Experiment with the crayon, rubbing with the side and the tip. The best images are made by rubbing the side of the crayon on the paper, not the tip. You may need to show your child how to use the side of the crayon, because children are often taught to use the tip of the crayon when they first start coloring.

What Your Child Is Learning

Crayon rubbings develop observation skills by encouraging children to look at, feel, and trace the objects in the rubbing. The goal of this activity is to study and describe the object. "What shape is it? Is it bumpy or smooth? Natural or man-made?" Introduce new vocabulary words like *trace* and *outline* plus adjectives that describe the objects you are using.

More Things to Do

Make new shapes for rubbings together: paper snowflakes for winter, hearts for Valentine's Day. Glue a rubbing to a piece of card stock to make a card for someone special!

Also for older children, make rubbings of things outside—tree bark, a manhole cover, a historic plaque, or the side of a building. Take a walk in your neighborhood with a crayon and paper and see what you can find. Remember to look up, down, and all around!

▶ Play a game with your child. Ask your child to feel the paper before she starts to color. Can she feel something underneath the paper? What shape is it? Can she trace the outline with her fingers? Can she guess what it might be?

Magical Mural Drawings

► AGES:	► ACTIVITY TIME:
2 to 4+ years	**15 to 30 minutes**

Materials

- a large piece of paper
- Water-soluble, washable markers or "jumbo" and "chunk-style" crayons* are recommended for children under three. Smaller crayons are better suited for children ages three and up.
- tape

Activity

Tape a large piece of paper to a tabletop or the bare floor. Provide four or five markers or crayons to draw with. If you are using markers with a young child, try giving her one at a time to prevent her from accidentally coloring on the table or floor.

Murals are exciting for children when there is a theme to explore. Lines are a good place to start, be-

*To make your own chunk-style crayons, see "How to Make Round Crayons," p. 213.

cause they are easy to draw. Also, there are so many variations and so many words to describe them. How many different kinds of lines can you draw? Fat, skinny, long, short, curved, zigzag, dotted, straight, crooked, and many more. You can talk about colors and shapes this way, too.

Older children three and up might enjoy choosing their own theme for a mural. If your child is having trouble coming up with an idea, suggest things that she knows well. Topics might include types of animals or the people in her family. When your child is done working on the mural, roll it up and save it for another day.

What Your Child Is Learning

People respond to murals because of the size. When artwork takes up a lot of space, it becomes part of a person's immediate environment. Hanging up a big drawing that your child made is a terrific way to make her feel loved. Also, because murals are large, they are traditionally a group project. Mural making is a chance for your child to work with you, other family members, or friends on a cooperative project, sharing the materials and making decisions about the design.

▶ Have you ever wondered how to talk to your child about her art? Ask your child to tell you about her artwork instead of trying to guess what it is. You may be surprised by her intricate explanations! It is fun to write down what she says and then display her stories along with her pictures. This is an excellent prereading activity.

More Things to Do

Just for fun, put on some music and act out some different kinds of lines, like tall (stand on tiptoes), short (squat down), bumpy (hop up and down), curvy (move like a snake), etc.

Make a mural with a group of kids! Make a circus the theme, or draw the alphabet starting with *A* is for —————, *B* is for —————, *C* is for —————, and so on.

Read your child a silly poem and have her draw a picture of her favorite part.

Have your child lie down on a piece of paper while you trace around her to make an outline. Color it in together.

Sticky Paper Collages

Materials

- ◆ clear contact paper (shelf paper), from a hardware or art supply store
- ◆ scrap materials with different colors and textures, like shiny paper, colored tissue, yarn, cotton balls, wrapping paper, magazine cuttings, felt or fabric, and sandpaper
- ◆ heavy paper or cardboard to use as a background
- ◆ masking tape

Activity

Peel the contact paper and tape it to a flat surface with the sticky side facing up. Before you start, show your child that the paper is sticky and let her experiment with what it feels like on her fingers.

Provide the child with a selection of materials to use. Keep the selection small to avoid dumping a whole basket of materials onto the paper. Encourage her to place different materials on the contact paper. Some materials can be peeled off and re-stuck. This can be an interesting way to rearrange the collage if your child likes to take things apart.

To save the picture when your child is finished, place a piece of paper roughly the same size or slightly larger on top of the sticky paper. Smooth down the paper, starting in one corner and working your way across the picture to eliminate air bubbles. Trim the edges with scissors.

What Your Child Is Learning

This is a sensory project designed to enhance your child's tactile sensibilities. She is learning to discriminate between different materials and to use words to describe their different properties. You can group the different materials you are using into two categories like "rough" and "smooth." Then, together, make a collage that combines materials from both categories.

More Things to Do

Make a stained-glass window! First make a sticky paper collage using materials that you can see through, like colored tissue paper or cellophane paper. Next, cut and peel another piece of shelf paper about the same size as the child's picture. Place the second sheet of sticky paper on top of the collage, sticky side down, so that the collage is in the middle. Tape it on a window.

Make a seasonal collage using leaves in the fall or flowers in the spring and summer. If you don't have time to collect leaves, make your own out of colored construction paper.

Include some photos in your collage!

Puzzle Play

▶ AGES:
9 months to 4+ years

▶ ACTIVITY TIME:
5 to 15 minutes

Materials

Ages nine months to one year
- a large wooden pegboard with ³/₄-inch- to 1-inch-diameter pegs
- containers like plastic pitchers, milk cartons, refrigerator containers, oatmeal boxes, or coffee cans for filling and emptying small objects

Ages one to two
- nesting cups
- a stacking pole
- shape and color sorters with wooden pegs
- a homemade box (see p. 139)

Ages two to three
- boxes with shapes cut out of the lid and matching shapes to fit inside
- puzzles where each piece has its own space, preferably with knobs

Ages three and up
- wooden jigsaw puzzles with between three and eight interlocking pieces
- a floor puzzle
- puzzles with pictures underneath that show where to place the pieces on top

Activity

Let your child practice with the appropriate activities in his age range. A lot of coordination and motor skills are needed to complete a puzzle, and these skills develop steadily as young children grow.

STACKABLE RINGS

SHAPE SORTERS

KNOB PUZZLES

JIGSAW PUZZLES

Activities like a stacking pole or nesting cups begin to develop and refine a very young child's motor skills and sense of size and shape relationships. Puzzle boxes let him discover that many objects can be made to fit through openings of various shapes. All of these skills will play an important role later on.

Your child will progress from these types of activities to being able to put together puzzles in which each individual piece has its own space. As he grows, he will be able to make connections between shapes in puzzles with interlocking pieces.

Remember that puzzles take patience. Give your child the time and space to try different combinations until he finds a way to make the pieces fit.

Through puzzle play, your child is making comparisons between the spaces where a piece will fit and the sizes and shapes of available pieces. Which piece is the biggest? Which piece is smallest? Which piece is round? How many pieces are there in all? All of these questions involve early math concepts.

What Your Child Is Learning

Puzzles emphasize shape recognition and connections between size and shape relationships. Puzzle play also teaches your child about patience, problem solving, and concentration skills as he devises different methods for maneuvering the pieces into place.

More Things to Do

Make a homemade puzzle box for ages one and two: Start with a plastic storage container or a coffee can with a plastic lid. Cut two or three basic shapes out of the lid, like a triangle, circle, and square. Your child can now fit objects such as blocks, large pop beads, spoons, or clothespins through the cut-out openings.

Look for *My First Book of Shapes* (by Gerald Murphy) at your bookstore or local library.

> ▶ Make a custom puzzle! Choose an interesting photograph, magazine, picture, or old calendar page. Cover the picture with clear contact paper and cut it into three to six simple shapes.

Paper Bag Puppets

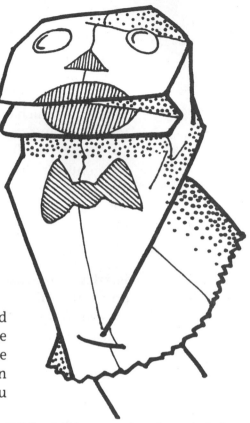

► **AGES:**
18 months to 4+ years

► **ACTIVITY TIME:**
10 to 30 minutes

Materials

- ◆ a paper lunch bag
- ◆ some or all of the following:
    markers, crayons, or oil pastels
    collage materials like scrap paper, tissue,
    yarn, felt, or fabric
    paste or glue and a paste brush*
    scissors

Activity

Show the child how to put the bag on his hand and make the flap move. The bottom flap on the bag will become the "mouth" or "face" of the puppet. You can fold the bottom of the bag in half, so that you can make a "mouth" that you can open and close with your fingers.

Set out the materials that you will be using. With children under three it is best to choose one medium: either color or collage. Older children may enjoy working with both drawing and collage materials at the same time.

Feel free to offer assistance or make suggestions as your child decorates the puppet, but let him make his own choices about how he decorates his bag. Your child may be too young to understand the whole concept behind making a puppet, but it is still a learning experience for him to be exposed to the process of using the materials.

*See "How to Make a Paste and Paint Brush," p. 210.

What Your Child Is Learning	Playing with paper bag puppets encourages your child to express himself with words and gestures. The puppet gives him the freedom to pretend. Making a puppet helps children recognize and describe different physical attributes. "My snake puppet has a long, thin tongue."
More Things to Do	Boost your child's creativity by talking to him about his puppet. Discuss the type of personality that the puppet will have. "Susie Snake has a long, thin body and no feet. She doesn't like eating spinach or green beans, but she loves to lie in the sun all day."

Work on your own puppet and when you are both finished, put on a play together.

For ages three and up: Decorate a paper grocery bag to create a mask that your child can wear. Cut eyeholes in one of the bag's flat faces, decorate with markers and collage materials. Add yarn for hair.

> *Parent quote:* The first time Eva made a puppet, she wouldn't let me help her with the face. She wanted to do the whole thing herself, just like with everything else. You couldn't really tell what it was when she was through, but she sure had a good time doing it."

Memory Game

► **AGES:** **2 to 4+ years**	► **ACTIVITY TIME:** **5 to 15 minutes**

Materials

- choose one of the following categories:
  small carpet sample squares (books of discontinued patterns are often available from rug stores)
  two identical stickers, file folder dots, or pieces of sandpaper, Mylar, cork, wallpaper, fabric, etc. (items should be flat)
- lightweight tagboard cut into 2-inch squares (two pieces for each material)
- glue
- scissors

Directions

This activity is a matching game using pairs. If you don't have two pieces of each material, cut the pieces in half. Material samples should be as close to two-inches square as possible so that they are large enough for your child to get a good look at them.

Choose pairs of different colors, patterns, or textures that are different enough for your child to be able to discriminate between them. Start with five pairs; you can always add more later. Glue these pairs to cardboard backings. Allow the glue to dry thoroughly before you play.

Activity	You may choose to start with only two or three of the pairs and as your child catches on, add more pairs to make it more complicated.

Activity — You may choose to start with only two or three of the pairs and as your child catches on, add more pairs to make it more complicated.

Show your child the cards you have made. Look at the pairs together and talk about what they look like and how they feel. "The carpet pieces are blue and fuzzy. The sandpaper is brown and rough."

Match the pairs with the cards faceup. Once she understands that the goal is to match like cards and she can locate the pairs, turn the cards over and play with the texture or pattern side facing down.

Take turns. The first player flips one card over, looks at the texture or pattern and tries to find its match in the pile of cards that remain.

When a match is made, the player gets to keep the pair. When there is no match, the cards are returned to the floor and turned upside down. A clever player will try to remember what cards she has seen and where they are located.

What Your Child Is Learning — This game gets its name because it builds concentration and memory skills. To play successfully, it requires that your child pay attention to the moves that both she and the other player make. Another challenge is to discriminate between like and unlike objects, making matches of pairs.

More Things to Do — **With children three and up:** Add more cards and play with the whole family!

Have one of the pairs correspond with a special prize. If your child finds the pair with the blue dots, she gets a little toy or favorite snack.

See "Puzzle Play," which also develops concentration and memory skills (p. 138).

▶ *Are you teaching your child about taking turns?*

This is a great game to teach your child about taking turns and game etiquette. Another game for young players is the card game Go Fish, which is also played with pairs. Use only a small part of the deck to keep things simple.

Go Fish

For ages three years and up.

Each player starts with a small hand. The remainder of the cards are facedown on the table.

Each player takes a turn asking a player for one of the cards he needs to make a match. If the player has this card, he gives it to him and the match is set aside. If the player doesn't have the card that is asked for, he tells the player to "go fish" in the card pile. The player chooses a card from the pile.

If there is a match, the player continues the turn, asking for another card, until there is no match. The winner is the player with the most pairs at the end of the game.

For beginners, remove pairs from a full deck and start with a hand with two or three cards in it and a small "fish pond."

Building Blocks

Materials

Ages one to two
- any of the following:
    alphabet blocks
    cloth-covered foam blocks
    nesting cups (colored plastic cups
    that fit inside each other)
    plastic tumblers
    Tupperware containers

Ages two to three
- any of the following:
    large interlocking plastic blocks like Duplo
    Star Builder sets
    empty shoe boxes or cereal boxes in many sizes
    empty yogurt containers with the lids taped down tightly
    small wooden blocks in a few basic shapes
    "beginner blocks" (the same shapes as wooden
    blocks but made out of foam)
    props like toy cars, animals, or people

Ages three to four
- any of the above plus:
    wooden blocks in many shapes
    Tinker Toys and Lincoln Logs

paper towel and toilet paper tubes and tin cans with smoothed edges
foam shapes (sold as a set or as factory surplus)

Ages four and up
♦ any of the above plus:
building sets with more pieces and smaller pieces like Lego
large building blocks made from cardboard
plastic or wooden spools
toy props

Activity

At ages one and two, children will learn about blocks through trial and error. By stacking them on top of each other and then knocking them down, they will learn about gravity. By laying them in straight rows, they will learn about straight lines and balance.

At ages two and three, children will learn how to create higher, sturdier, and more visually appealing stacks of blocks. They enjoy putting blocks that are similar together, and making long lines and sharp corners. They imagine that their constructions are fanciful "castles."

You will notice that the difference in block play with children **ages three and four** lies in what they do with the blocks themselves rather than a need for more sophisticated playthings. Although they can manipulate small interlocking pieces, like Legos, they are often content designing intricate structures with toys recommended for younger ages.

The parent's role in block play is to find a balance between demonstrating new ideas and allowing your child to figure things out on her own. If a structure falls down, help your child develop problem-solving strategies to correct it. Show her how to build a broader base, stack units more exactly, or use larger units on the bottom and smaller ones on the top.

What Your Child Is Learning

Blocks are an exercise in design and creativity. Through block play, children employ many skills, including: sorting according to shape and size, forming straight lines and sharp corners, using vertical or horizontal placement, using stacking and balance, and creating patterns. The spirit of block play is experimentation through trial and error. Block structures also provide a rich setting for imaginary play.

More Things to Do

Together make a tower as tall as your child!

For children ages three and up: Build an environment with large blocks made out of shoe boxes, folded cardboard blocks, or lightweight plastic (like BRIK blocks). Blocks this size challenge children to build a structure big enough for them to play inside of.

▶ *What kind of block set can I buy for my eighteen-month-old?*

Corrugated cardboard blocks are good for very young children who like to knock things over. Because the blocks are light and don't have sharp edges, they are safe for young ones to play with. Plus, cardboard blocks are sturdy, inexpensive, and can be used to build things for years to come.

Like all good toys, blocks grow with your child. The way your child uses blocks changes as she grows.

▶ *Where could I get fifty shoe boxes?*

Many shoe stores have lots of extra boxes. All you have to do is ask—you could be one phone call away from a gold mine. When you pick them up, bring bags along with you to carry them home.

CHAPTER 6

Music and Movement

Hello, Hello

Tune: a rap, chant, or song of your own

Song

Hello, hello, hello, hello
Hello to Jenny, hello, hello

Bonjour, bonjour, bonjour, bonjour (French)
Bonjour to Julia, bonjour, bonjour

Hola, hola, hola, hola (Spanish)
Hola to Miguel, hola, hola

Shalom, shalom, shalom shalom
(Hebrew)
Shalom to Quinton, shalom

What Your Child Is Learning

"Hello, Hello" begins to introduce your child to the idea that people come from many different places and speak many different languages. Exposure to different languages develops sound discrimination and listening skills. Learning about people from other countries shows children similarities and differences between cultures and promotes tolerance.

Open Them and Shut Them

Tune: a chant or rap of your own

Start with your hands in front of you.

**Song and
Movements**

Open them and shut them   (open and close your fists)
Open them and shut them
Give a little clap   (clap your hands)

Open them and shut them
Open them and shut them
Lay them in your lap   (place your hands in your lap)

Creep them, creep them
Way up to your chin   (walk your fingers from your lap to your chin)
Open up your little mouth   (open your mouth)
But do not let them in

Open them and shut them
Open them and shut them
To your shoulders fly   (fly your hands to your shoulders)
Then like little birdies
Let them flutter to the sky   (flutter your hands and arms to the sky)

Falling, falling, falling   (your arms flutter down)
Almost to the ground
Quickly pick them up again
And turn them round and round   (circle your hands around each other in a
                                                  spinning motion)

Faster, faster, faster   (circle quickly)
Slower, slower, slower   (circle slower)
Stop!   (clap your hands)

What Your Child Is Learning   This traditional finger play is a wonderful tension release. It is a playful way to teach children to identify different body parts and promote body awareness, all within the framework of a rhyme.

Now I'm Going Forward

Tune: your own chant or rap

Song and Movements

Now I'm going forward, forward, forward   (walk forward)
Now I'm going forward
Come with me

Chorus
Now I'm going up and down   (first up on tip-
Up and down, up and down   toe, then bend
Now I'm going up and down   your knees)
Turn around with me

Now I'm going backward, backward, backward (walk backward)
Now I'm going backward
Come with me

(Chorus)

Now I'm going sideways, sideways, sideways   (walk sideways)
Now I'm going sideways
Come along with me

(Chorus)

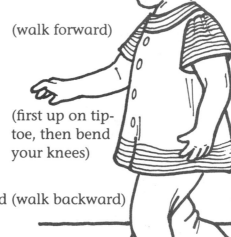

What Your Child Is Learning

Your child is learning directions through movement. He is practicing moving up and down, forward and back, and sideways. As he learns to describe his movements using directional words, he is also refining his coordination skills.

Walking, Walking

Tune: "Frère Jacques"

Sit in a cross-legged position. Use your fingers to make the movements. After you have sung the song with finger plays, sing it again while moving around the room.

Song and Movements

Walking, walking Walking, walking	(second and third fingers walk in the air)
Hop, hop, hop Hop, hop, hop	(make your fingers hop)
Running, running, running Running, running, running	(make your fingers run up and down)
Now let's stop Now let's stop	(freeze on stop)

After stopping, ask your child to make a high shape, a low shape, and a medium shape with her body. A high shape might be on tippy-toe, arms outstretched. A low shape could be close to the ground or on the floor. A medium shape is somewhere between high and low. Can you balance on one leg? On the other? Can the two of you make a shape together? Ask her to find an ending shape, any shape she chooses. Hold it!

What Your Child Is Learning

Your child is practicing locomotion: walking, running, and hopping. She is developing balance and flexibility while sharpening her listening skills and ability to follow directions. And all of this is happening in the guise of a game.

Point to the Window

Tune: a chant, rap, or song of your own

After you sing each line of the song, do what it tells you to do.

Song and Movements

Point to the window
Point to the door
Point to the ceiling
Point to the floor

Clap to the window
Clap to the door
Clap to the ceiling
Clap to the floor

Walk to the window
Walk to the door
Walk to the ceiling   (use your hands to walk up to the ceiling)
Walk to the floor   (use your hands to walk down to the floor)

Run to the window, etc.

What Your Child Is Learning

What an enjoyable way to exercise and gain coordination! This game teaches the movements of pointing and clapping as well as object identification, with a sense of humor.

I'm Tall, I'm Small

Tune: a chant, rap, or song of your own

Begin by sitting on the floor in a cross-legged position.

Song and Movements

I'm stretching very tall   (stretch your arms over your head)
And now I'm very small   (stretch down, curved in)
I'm tall, I'm small   (stretch up and down)
I'm a little ball   (body curled down in a ball)

I'm stretching very high   (stretch your arms over your head)
And now I'm very low   (stretch down low)
I'm high, I'm low   (stretch high)
No place else to go   (stretch high, stretch low)

(Repeat the song and movements, first slowly, then quickly.)

What Your Child Is Learning

Your child is experiencing the concept of opposites: tall and small, high and low, fast and slow. Through stretching and curling he is learning kinesthetically.

Dancing with Scarves

Materials
- scarves
- lyrical music of your choice

Activity

Put the music on. Move around the room, using the scarves any way you please.

After a few minutes, lower the music. Observe your child. What interesting movements is he making? Make specific comments about his movements like, "I like the way you're swinging your scarf. Can you hide your face behind it? Are you playing peekaboo?"

Make suggestions at first. Can he hold the scarf in one hand? Can he change to the other hand? Throw the scarf into the air. Let it fall down. Throw the scarf in the air again. Can he catch it? Ask him if he has any ideas. Eventually, he will have many. Follow his movements.

Together, walk with your scarves. Run. Slide. Freeze.

Ask your child to use his body to make a high shape, low shape, and medium shape.

A high shape could be on tippy-toe or with his arms outstretched. A low shape is close to the ground. A medium shape would be somewhere in between. Connect with each other and find an ending shape. Ask him to pose with you when you say "Freeze."

What Your Child Is Learning

Using props such as scarves increases your child's awareness of the properties of different materials. Children tend to feel more secure if they have something to hold on to while they move. Scarves are light and soft and float gently to the ground. Expand his vocabulary by describing his actions with as much detail as possible.

More Things to Do

Use other props: a big round ball, streamer bracelets, Mylar, artificial flowers, feather boas, pom-poms, hula hoops, or wooden rhythm sticks that lend themselves to other kinds of movement. Talk about how these props look and feel. With a variety of music, explore the movement possibilities of each material.

Stop and Go! Make a Shape

Materials
- a drum, tambourine, or marching music

Activity

Beat the drum in a steady rhythm. Invite your child to move around the room to the beat. When the drum stops, your child will stop and freeze, wherever he is, in a shape.

Repeat the activity many times, until your child gets the idea. Practice freezing in different body shapes and movements. Reach up to make a high shape, reach down to make a low shape. Practice an in-between or medium shape. Walk faster. Walk slower. Walk on tiptoe.

What Your Child Is Learning

This activity combines listening skills with physical exercise and body awareness. Your child is learning to follow directions as she moves and "freezes" around the room. Body control, balance, and flexibility influence what her body can do as she makes different shapes with her arms, legs, torso, neck, and head.

One, Two, Three, Four

Tune: your own chant or rap

Song and Movements

One, two, three, four
See me walk along the floor   (walk around the room)

Five, six, seven, eight
See me walking nice and straight   (walk on tiptoe)

Walk to the front and say "hi"   (walk forward, say "hi")
Walk to the back and say "bye"   (walk backward, say "bye")

Walk to the right and say "woo"   (walk right, say "woo")
Walk to the left and say "boo"   (walk left, say "boo")

(Repeat)

What Your Child Is Learning

"One, Two, Three, Four" is an exercise song that promotes self-esteem through successful listening. Your child must pay careful attention to the words of the song to hear what she is expected to do next. If she listens, she'll see that the directions are easy to follow. This song also presents the concepts of right and left, front and back, and the numbers one through eight.

Old MacDonald Had a Band

Tune: "Old MacDonald Had a Farm"

Materials

♦ a tambourine, drum, cymbal, triangle
(and other instruments if you have them)

Song and Movements

Old MacDonald had a band
E—I—E—I—O
And in this band he had a *tambourine*
E—I—E—I—O

With a *jingle jangle* here
And a *jingle jangle* there
Here a *jingle*
There a *jangle*
Everywhere a *jingle jangle*
Old MacDonald had a band
E—I—E—I—O

Repeat the song with other instruments, for example:

Drums—Boom boom
Cymbal—Cling clang
Triangle—Plink plink

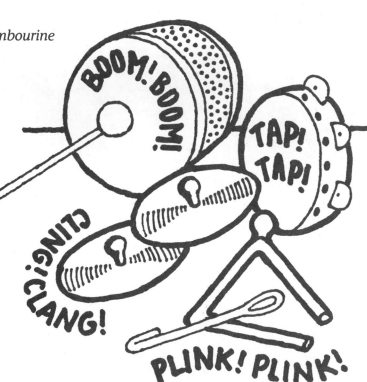

What Your Child Is Learning

Your child is learning the names and sounds of various instruments. Also, this song introduces her to the idea of rhythm and that instruments are played in rhythm with a song. Learning to identify individual instruments and their sounds builds appreciation for an understanding of music. Because this song is a spin-off of the traditional song "Old MacDonald," it may inspire her to make up some of her own lyrics to a familiar tune.

Making Music

Materials

- homemade instruments:
a tightly sealed coffee can
filled with dried beans; a
musical shaker (see p. 165);
pots and pans of various
sizes and a wooden spoon
- store-bought instruments:
bells, maracas, a drum, cymbals,
a wood block, rhythm sticks

Activity

Lay out the various instruments. Invite your child to experiment with the instruments and see what kinds of sounds they make.

Introduce the words *loud* and *soft*. Can she make both loud and soft sounds with each instrument? What do the sounds remind her of? Drums may sound like thunder or chimes may sound like rain.

Play along with your voice, a tape, or the radio. Dress up and parade around the room!

What Your Child Is Learning

Sound, along with the other senses, is an important element in a preschooler's development. Because they are natural noisemakers, preschoolers can be taught to use rhythm and sound as a means of expression. Music can be a powerful medium for developing your child's self-esteem.

More Things to Do

Start a collection of instruments. Costs can be kept to a minimum. Look for instruments from around the world like the Chinese drum, a kalimba from Africa, or a rain stick from South America.

Make some sand blocks! You'll need two small wooden blocks, some sandpaper, and white glue. Cut the sandpaper to fit the size of the wood blocks, so that a piece of sandpaper wraps around each block. Glue the sandpaper to the wood with white glue. Rub the blocks together to make a scratching sound.

Musical Shakers

For ages eighteen months to four years and up.

Materials

- ◆ two disposable plates
- ◆ dried beans
- ◆ a stapler
- ◆ colorful paper shapes and streamers or stickers (optional)
- ◆ glue or paste and a brush for use with decorations (optional)

Activity

Place one plate on the work surface, faceup. Ask your child to put a small handful of dried beans on the plate. Children who are still putting things in their mouths will need to be carefully supervised while the shaker is being assembled or played with.

Next, place the other plate on top of the one with the beans, facedown so that the beans are sandwiched between the two plates. Staple the plates together along the edges. Be careful to keep the staples close together so that the beans won't fall out.

Your child may decorate the plate by gluing on colorful streamers or shapes. Stickers are also fun and can be used to attach streamers to the edges. To do this, use the sticker as you would a piece of tape.

Use the shaker while singing a favorite song or listening to a favorite tape.

| What Your Child Is Learning | Music appreciation and self-expression start early. Shakers develop rhythm, teach your child to discriminate between different sounds, and encourage expressive movement. Explore together the ideas of "loud" and "soft" and "fast" and "slow." See what types of movements the two of you can make to the rhythm. |

| More Things to Do | Make a shaker out of a toilet paper or paper towel roll. Cover one end of the roll with a piece of waxed paper and a rubber band. Put the beans or plastic poker chips into the tube. Cover the other end with more wax paper and another rubber band. Shake! |

Ages two and a half and up: Make your child a tambourine! You will need a sturdy disposable plate, a hole punch, string, and sixteen large buttons. Punch four holes in the plate, equidistant, around the edge of the plate. Thread a piece of string through each of the holes. String four buttons onto each string. Tie the ends of the string together so that they form a loop. Shake!

▶ *Inexpensive instruments (under ten dollars):*

Sleigh bells, jingle bells, fife, castanets, maracas, plastic harmonica, rhythm sticks, cymbals, triangle, whistle, kazoo, kalimba

CHAPTER 7
Pretend Play

Funny Face Painting

Materials

- face paints: either water-soluble crayons like Caran d'Ache or a children's watercolor paint set and a small brush with a long handle (both are available at art supply, craft, and toy stores). Use the "cake" type of watercolors for this project.
- a mirror
- a small container of water (to dip crayons or the brush in)
- paper towels (to wipe off crayons or the brush)
- water, soap, and a towel for washing
- liquid dishwashing soap to add when using watercolors (optional)

Activity

In Playspace, we use water-soluble crayons. They are colorful, easy to apply and remove, and can be sharpened for detailed work. Simply dip them in water to soften them up and you are ready to go.

Another option is to use a watercolor paint set. The colors come in small cakes that are easily mixed with water. Add a drop of liquid soap to a wet brush before painting with watercolors. It will make the paint easier to wash off later.

To begin, seat the child at a height that is comfortable for you. Set the container with water and a paper towel close by. Include a hand mirror so that your child can see his face as it is being painted.

Young children may have a hard time sitting still and are not used to the feeling of paint on their skin. A simple design like a heart, flower, or rainbow will suffice. It's a good idea to offer three designs and ask him to choose one. If your child appears to be uncomfortable with face painting, he may enjoy having you paint a design on his hand instead.

Older children may want more paint on their faces or may ask to have a specific animal or character painted. Use the hand mirror with older children so that they can watch and give directions.

What Your Child Is Learning

Changing your child's outward appearance through face painting can be a powerful experience for him because in childhood there is a thin line between fantasy and reality. Transforming your child into his favorite animal or character for an afternoon can be a tremendous boost for his self-esteem. Often, face painting doesn't have to be anything elaborate, just the small touch of painting a star, heart, or rainbow on a child's face is enough to make him feel really special.

More Things to Do

Add hats, accessories, or dress-up clothes to enhance pretend play.

Put on some music and have a parade!

Dress-Up and Pretend

Materials

For Dress-Up
- adult-sized clothes: dresses, coats, or pants (items may need to be shortened, either by simply cutting them with scissors or hemming them if they are bulky or too long)
- shoes and hats
- a purse, a briefcase, small suitcase, or sturdy shopping bag
- large plastic bracelets, necklaces, and other jewelry that is safe for toddlers
- a full-length mirror (shatterproof glass, if possible)

For Pretend
- telephones, toy dishes, kitchen utensils, medical kits, toy tools, a feather duster, small broom and dustpan, etc.

Activity

Provide your child with the dress-up clothes and accessories. Place the mirror close by. What would your child like to wear? Would she like to pretend to be somebody special? You can dress up, too, and let your child lead you through a play scenario.

Pay close attention to what she chooses to wear or carry. These clues can help you start a conversation. If she is carrying a purse or a suitcase, ask her about where she is going. Would she mind picking up a few things for you from the store? Ask her to make you something to eat. Encourage her to look at herself in the mirror and enjoy the experience.

Children love to pretend to be almost anything, but the most fun of all is pretending to be a grown-up.

What Your Child Is Learning

Children practice for adulthood and the responsibilities that come with growing up through dress-up and pretend play. Trying on adult roles is appealing to them because it lets them explore possibilities of who they would like to be. Dressing up is a way for kids to imitate adults at work—firemen, doctors, teachers, or policemen. Firemen wear hats and ride in big red engines to put out fires. Doctors help sick people to feel better. Teachers show kids how to read.

More Things to Do

For toddlers, putting on and taking off a hat can be an activity in itself. Use the words *on* and *off* as the two of you play together.

Use more props! A tea set, a baby doll and a blanket, or an old set of keys will provide material for more scenarios.

To make your child a play environment, see "How to Make a Box House," p. 225.

> ▶ As all parents know, the things you say may come back to you at the funniest times. Don't be surprised if you hear your child repeating to another child instructions you have given to her, like, "Shhh, you have to be quiet because the baby's taking a nap."

Small World Play

Materials

♦ **Ages two to four:** a dollhouse, farm, circus, or other play environment with people, cars, dinosaurs, animals, tractors, and other props, either store bought or homemade.

♦ **Additional building materials for ages three and up:** small blocks, small boxes, empty containers, play dough* or plasticene clay**, cotton balls, colored construction paper, small twigs, scissors, glue

Activity

Introduce your child to the toys and building materials you have chosen. Use this opportunity to help your child stretch his imagination. A small twig in a ball of plasticene can become a tree. A box lined with cotton balls can be a snowy field. A yogurt container can be a bear's warm cave.

She can use her plastic

*See our recipes for play dough, p. 50.
**Plasticene clay is available at art supply, craft, and toy stores.

animals to begin a stream-of-consciousness scene: the bear wakes up in its warm cave and decides to go out for a walk in the snowy field. Who does the bear see there but a bunny rabbit. The bear says to the bunny rabbit, where did you get those long ears? . . .

Usually, a child will need very little introduction to the materials before she will initiate her own play scenario. Relax and let her develop a theme. Ask your child to tell you a story about her play scene.

Older children three and up enjoy constructing elaborate environments, while younger children will be content with a simple box or block structure. Dollhouses or play farms with doors are also fun for children who are mastering the mechanics of opening, closing, and latching.

If you are making your own construction, build it in a quiet place where it will not be in the way. Your child may want to play with it for a few days.

What Your Child Is Learning

Why are kids so interested in miniature settings? Children create fantasy worlds so that they can have a place to act out scenes about people they know and things they've seen. In this way, your child can internalize her experiences.

> ▶ *Can I use pretend play as a way to talk to my child about real situations?*
>
> Yes. Pretending can be an excellent way to talk about situations that could be stressful for your child. Big changes like a new baby, moving, or starting school or day care can all be tough transitions for young kids. Using puppets to act out roles of important players can help her to think through what will happen. "You be the new teacher and I'll be the new student. Hello, and welcome to our class. Would you like to sing a song with us?" By practicing what to expect, she can alleviate some of her fears and be better prepared for a new situation.

More Things to Do

Ages two and a half and up: Make a whole village from play dough! Play dough is perfect for building houses, people, and animals. Use the "uncooked" recipe and bake the pieces to make them longer lasting. The play dough pieces can be painted with watercolors or tempera paint.

A reading readiness activity: Write down your child's story. Print the story in large letters on a big piece of paper and read it together. Take a picture of her play scene to keep with the story.

Here's a Ball for Baby

Tune: a chant, rap, or song of your own

Song and Movements

Here's a ball for baby
Big and fat and round   (make a big ball shape with your arms in front of you)
Here is baby's hammer
See how it can pound   (make two fists and bang one on top of the other)

Here are baby's soldiers
Standing in a row   (hold up the fingers of both hands)
Here is baby's music
clapping, clapping so   (clap your hands together)

Here is baby's trumpet
Toot, toot, toot, toot, toot   (blow air through your fists)
Here's the way that baby
Plays peekaboo   (hide your face behind your hands, show your face on "boo")

Here's a big umbrella
To keep the baby dry   (your hands meet over your head)
Here is my baby's cradle
Rock a baby bye   (make a cradle with your arms and rock)

What Your Child Is Learning

This song focuses on your child's concentration skills using a sequence of words and movements. Because the hand and finger movements are very descriptive, she will enjoy trying to remember which action comes next. A wonderful song for fun and pantomime!

Animal Dances

Tune: "Eensy-Weensy Spider" (the first four lines)

Song

The eensy-weensy spider
Went up the water spout
Down came the rain
And washed the spider out

Materials

♦ pictures of a kitten, rabbit, elephant, dog,
and fish for children to identify who
they are and how they move

Activity

First do the movements with your hands and fingers, while
singing the song. Initially, do this sitting in one place. Then,
move around the room, using your whole body and singing.

**Song and
Movements**

I am a little kitty
I love to tippy-toe
Won't you do it with me
Ready, now let's go
Tiptoe, tiptoe
Tiptoe, tiptoe, tiptoe   (tiptoe around the room)

I am a little rabbit
I love to hippy hop
Won't you do it with me
It's fun, we'll never stop

Hip hop, hip hop
Hip hop, hip hop, hip hop   (hop around the room)

I am a great big elephant
I take big steps so slow
Won't you do it with me
Ready now, let's go
So slow, so slow   (use your arms to make a
So slow, so slow, so slow   trunk, walk slowly and
                                   heavily around the room)

I am a little dog
I love to run and run
Won't you do it with me
We could have such fun
Let's run, let's run
Let's run, let's run, let's run   (run around the room)

I am a little fish
I love to swim and swim
Join me in the water
Ready now, jump in
We'll swim, we'll swim   (place your palms
We'll swim, we'll swim, we'll swim together and swim
                                   around the room)

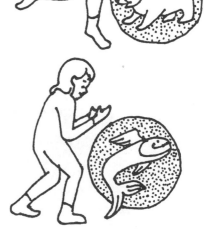

**What Your
Child Is
Learning**

"Animal Dances" teach animal identification
through rhyme, repetitions, and pantomime. Songs
that use rhyme and repetition of words favor sound-
discrimination skills and demonstrate the musical
qualities of language.

**More Things
to Do**

Make up words that describe a giraffe, peacock, frog,
inchworm, owl, or flamingo.

Jack in the Box

Begin the poem in a standing position. Follow the movements as you recite the poem.

Poem and Movements

Jack in the box Sits so still	(roll down into a ball with your hands covering your head)
Will he come out Yes he will!	(burst out of the ball into a standing position with your arms extended upward)

(Repeat many times)

What Your Child Is Learning

This poem is a fantastic way for your child to get the wiggles out. The waiting time that is built in to the movements fosters impulse control. The ending of the poem allows the release of tension. The coordination needed to execute the motions builds balance and flexibility.

Mask Making

▶ AGES:
18 months to 4+ years

▶ ACTIVITY TIME:
10 to 20 minutes

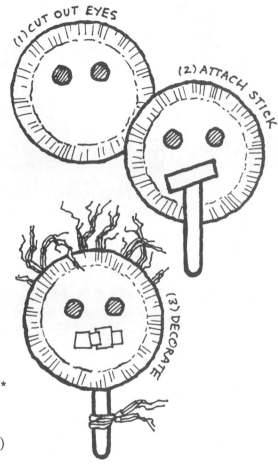

Materials

- a paper plate
- a Popsicle (craft) stick*
- scissors
- masking tape
- choose one category from the following materials for decorating:
    - markers, crayons or oil pastels
    - collage materials like construction paper, colored tissue, wrapping paper, or Mylar
- glue or paste and a brush (for collage)**
- yarn for hair (optional)
- feathers,* paper cut into streamers, raffia* (optional)
- for children over age three with parent supervision: sequins* or glitter* (optional)

Activity

Ahead of time, cut two circles in the paper plate for eyes with scissors. Attach the Popsicle or craft stick to the back of the plate with masking tape.

Set out the materials so that they are within reach of your child. She can design her mask any way that she chooses.

*Available at art and craft supply stores.
**See "How to Make a Paste and Paint Brush," p. 210.

Young children may not make the connection between decorating and creating a mask. Older children can be very elaborate, using yarn or straw for hair or paper shapes for eyebrows. As a finishing touch, streamers, raffia, or feathers can be attached with glue.

What Your Child Is Learning

Masks transform the familiar sight of your own image in the mirror into something new. Once a child puts on a mask, she is no longer herself. She is free to be whoever she wants to be. Playacting with masks is a valuable way for your child to act out feelings and situations in a healthy way.

More Things to Do

With ages three and up: Make a paper bag mask! You will need a large paper grocery bag and materials for decorating. First, with scissors cut two eyeholes on one side of the bag, so that she can see when she is wearing it. You may cut out a shape for the mouth too, if you wish. Decorate with drawing or collage materials.

> ▶ There is an element of discovery and surprise that comes when your child puts on a mask to play. She may see a new side of herself as she uses her imagination in new ways.

Stick Puppets

▶ AGES:
18 months to 4+ years

▶ ACTIVITY TIME:
5 to 15 minutes

Materials

- lightweight cardboard like oaktag or posterboard (available at art or craft supply stores)
- a pen or a pencil
- scissors
- animal stencils (optional)
- a straw or unsharpened pencil
- tape
- collage materials for decorating: paper scraps, colored tissue, Mylar, wrapping paper, yarn, cotton balls
- paste or glue and a brush*

Activity

Trace an animal shape on the board with a pencil, either by hand or using a stencil. This is free-form—use whichever method is comfortable for you. The animal can be quite simple. Make sure that the shape is large enough for your child to decorate easily. Cut out the animal shape with scissors.

Lay out the decorating materials that you will be using. The more whimsical the materials are, the better. Bits of brightly colored paper for eyes, cotton balls for cheeks, and scraps of fabric or yarn add personality to the finished puppet.

Present your child with the animal cut-out, decorating materials, and glue. He

*See "How to Make a Paste and Paint Brush," p. 210.

can choose pieces of collage materials that are interesting to him and glue them to the animal shape.

With young children, this activity is more of an exercise in pasting and hand-eye coordination than in creating a puppet with a persona. This is okay. With older children, this activity is about making choices about colors and shapes and using them to invent a puppet with a unique personality. "Sammy the squirrel has a long, bushy, brown tail."

When your child has finished with decorating, tape a straw or unsharpened pencil to the back of the animal shape. Ask him to put on a puppet show for you!

What Your Child Is Learning

Playing with stick puppets exercises hand-eye coordination and encourages your child to explore expression through movement. Making the puppet itself develops aesthetic sensibilities. The characters created are fun and fanciful, but the person holding a puppet infuses it with a personality that comes from his imagination alone.

▶ *How do you draw animals?*

When you are drawing animals, think about breaking them down into simple shapes like triangles, circles, and squares. This will make drawing easier. It works for drawing other things, too.

▶ Mary Dunsay, our Playspace volunteer, says, "I use cookie cutters as stencils to get around drawing. I just trace around the outside of the cutter with a pencil and cut out the shape. Then I put a few pieces of paper underneath the one with the outlines, so that I can cut out lots of shapes at one time. Shortcuts like these are real time savers."

More Things to Do

Your new puppet is perfect for "Shadow Shows," an activity about light and shadow (see the next project). For an evening of fun, older children may want to make a few different puppets to use as characters in a shadow play.

Make some stage props for your puppet characters. Make a dancing tree on a stick, the sun, or some clouds. Garden stakes can be attached to larger items with tape so that the props are movable like the puppets.

Shadow Shows

► AGES:
18 months to 4+ years

► ACTIVITY TIME:
10 to 20 minutes

Materials

♦ a large flashlight or gooseneck lamp
♦ a blank wall or sheet tacked to a wall
♦ any of the following:
    familiar shapes like circles or
    triangles, animals, flowers, etc.,
    cut from heavy paper and taped to Popsicle
    (craft) sticks, straws, or unsharpened pencils
    hand puppets
    small stuffed animals

Activity

Close the curtains and turn out the lights. Set up the flashlight or lamp so that the light shines directly onto the sheet or blank wall, illuminating the area.

Entice your child to join you in playing in front of the light, making shadows with your bodies and hands. Can she move fast like a rabbit? Slow like a turtle?

Next, introduce the paper shapes, puppets, or stuffed animals. Hold them in front of the light, so that their shadows are projected on to the blank wall. Can she name the object? How did she know what it was? Do the shadows change as the object moves closer to or farther away from the light?

With older children, show them how to make different animal shapes with their hands. Can your child make a bunny? Can she make the bunny hop?

What Your Child Is Learning

What makes a shadow? If she moves does her shadow move with her? What kinds of shadows can she make with her hands? What objects can she identify by their shadows? Light and shadow are mesmerizing because shadow makes the ordinary appear mysterious.

More Things to Do

Once your child can name all of the shapes, play a game of What's My Name? Ask your child to choose one of the shapes and place it in front of the light. You guess the name of the object she chose. Next, you pick an object so that she can guess.

On a sunny day, take your shadows outside and see what kinds of shapes the two of you can make on the ground.

For children over three: Take apart a flashlight to see what's inside. How does it work? The batteries inside it generate light for the lightbulb. Can she put it back together?

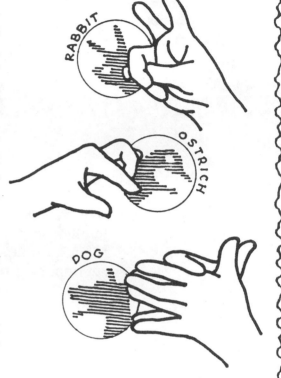

RABBIT

OSTRICH

DOG

CHAPTER 8

Cooking

Peanut Butter

Ingredients and Supplies

- peanuts
- a blender or food processor
- cooking oil
- honey (for children eighteen months and older)*
- salt to taste (optional)
- a measuring cup and measuring spoons
- a flexible cake spatula or spoon

(1) ADD PEANUTS, OIL AND HONEY

(2) BLEND ON LOW

(3) ADD SALT

Recipe

Measure 1 cup of peanuts and pour them into the blender or food processor. Mix the peanuts on a low speed. Add 4 tablespoons of cooking oil and 1 tablespoon of honey. Blend on low. Your child can help you measure and work the blender.

*For information about honey and young children, see "Snack Collage," p. 194.

If the mixture seems too thick to blend thoroughly, add more oil ¹/₂ teaspoon at a time. Also, if the peanut butter sticks to the sides of the blender, remove it with a cake spatula or spoon. Add salt to taste after the mixture is blended. Serve on a cracker or piece of bread.

What Your Child Is Learning

Homemade peanut butter is a new taste sensation for most kids who are used to more processed store-bought varieties. This peanut butter recipe will involve your child in following directions, observing the changes that occur when food is blended, and in the process solving the mystery of how peanut butter is made. The best feeling is the satisfaction that comes from making something yourself!

More Things to Do

Eat peanut butter on a banana, apple, or celery stick!

Buy some peanuts that are still in the shell.

See instructions for making "Homemade Butter," p. 190

Homemade Butter

▶ AGES:	▶ ACTIVITY TIME:
2 to 4+ years	**5 to 10 minutes**

Ingredients and Supplies

- small glass jars with lids—baby food jars are perfect
- 1 pint heavy cream
- a large bowl of ice
- crackers and a knife

Note: Plastic jars do not work as well as glass for this activity.

Recipe

Chill the heavy cream in a bowl of ice. The trick to making homemade butter quickly is to keep the cream very cold. Another option is to put the cream in the freezer shortly before you are ready to start.

Fill the jar half full of cream. Make sure the lid is on tight! Shake the jar for about five minutes or until butter has formed inside the jar.

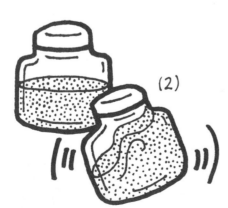

Soon you will feel the cream changing. First it will thicken. Next you will feel a lump in the center of the jar and then a chunk of butter will form. Open the jar as you go along to check your progress. You and your child can take turns shaking the butter so that you don't get tired.

Spread your finished butter on a cracker and enjoy!

What Your Child Is Learning

Butter is an excellent example of how a food can change form. This simple recipe can give your child a real sense of accomplishment, along with the knowledge of how butter is made. Sweet-cream butter may also be a new taste sensation for many children who are used to eating the salted variety.

More Things to Do

Spread your butter on whole wheat bread!

Make homemade whipped cream. Use whipping cream and a beater. You may add a sprinkle of sugar to taste. Serve with fresh berries, bananas, or your favorite ice cream.

Applesauce

► AGES:
18 months to 4+ years

► ACTIVITY TIME:
about 45 minutes

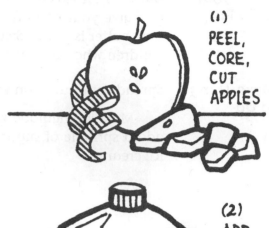

(1)
PEEL,
CORE,
CUT
APPLES

Ingredients and Supplies

- apples, minimum one per person
- sugar
- cinnamon
- a large saucepan with a lid
- water
- measuring spoons
- a peeler or paring knife
- cutting board
- potato masher or fork

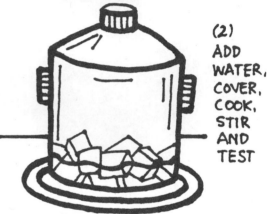

(2)
ADD
WATER,
COVER,
COOK,
STIR
AND
TEST

Recipe

Peel the apples, core them, and cut them into quarters. Then cut each quarter into three or four bite-size pieces. Place all of the apple pieces in a large saucepan.

Older children will be able to help you with each step of the process, starting with peeling the apples. Younger children may not be able to peel and core the apples but may be able to help you cut up quartered sections into small pieces with a plastic knife.

Add 1 tablespoon of water to the pot for each apple you used. Cover and cook the apples over low heat for fifteen to twenty minutes, stirring occasionally until the apples are soft enough to be mashed. Test apples for softness with a fork.

Your child can also help you measure the water and the sugar. Don't measure over the pot, in case there is a spill. Instead, measure water and sugar over the sink

(3) ADD SUGAR + COOK MORE + MASH APPLES + ADD CINNAMON

or over an empty bowl. Ingredients can be poured into a small plastic container and then transferred to the saucepan.

When the apples are ready, add 1 tablespoon of sugar for each apple in the recipe. Stir well. Cover and cook for a few more minutes.

Mash apples with a fork or potato masher. Sprinkle with cinnamon to taste. Applesauce may be served warm or cold.

What Your Child Is Learning

This recipe lets your child compare raw apples to cooked ones. How do the apples change? Peeling and cutting build your child's small motor skills and at the same time show her the proper use of kitchen utensils. She can learn to cut the apples with a blunt knife and to use a peeler and a potato masher. By measuring the water and sugar in proportion to the number of apples, she begins to see that recipes are based on relationships between ingredients.

More Things to Do

Learn the new vocabulary words "peel" and "mash."

Try applesauce chunky or smooth.

Put applesauce on cinnamon toast!

Snack Collage

▶ **AGES:**
18 months to 4+ years

▶ **ACTIVITY TIME:**
10 to 15 minutes

Ingredients and Supplies

- Cheerios
- honey*
- a Popsicle (craft) stick
- a small paper plate
- a Dixie cup
- apple or banana slices, raisins (optional)
- a wet cloth

Recipe

Give your child a paper plate with a teaspoon of honey on it and a craft stick. Show her how to use the stick to draw a design with the honey on her paper plate. She can draw lines, circles, or the first letter of her name.

Fill a Dixie cup with Cheerios. She can use the honey like glue to stick and Cheerios to the paper plate. The result is a collage that she can eat for a snack.

Include other foods. Cut each item into bite-size pieces and put it in its own Dixie cup.

*Honey is dangerous for children under a year old, because it carries a risk of botulism. This information is from the Centers for Disease Control as cited in *Pregnancy and Childbirth,* by Tracy Hotchner (Avon Books, updated 1990).

When she's done creating, she can eat her snack with her fingers. Clean up messy hands with a wet cloth.

What Your Child Is Learning

Make an ordinary snack extraordinary! The ingredients allow her to try new tastes and combinations of foods. Most of all, she will love that she made it all by herself!

More Things to Do

Spread some honey on a warm biscuit or piece of toast.

Make applesauce! See our recipe, p. 192.

Bangaroo Banana Shakes

Ingredients and Supplies

- ◆ 1¹/₃ cups milk
- ◆ 2 bananas
- ◆ a blender
- ◆ individual cups

Recipe

Ask your child to help by peeling or helping you peel the bananas. If he is old enough, he may cut the bananas into small pieces with a plastic knife. He can also help you measure and pour the milk.

Combine the bananas and milk in the blender. Blend at medium speed, to any desired thickness. Ask your child to push the button on the blender to whip the shakes, and press the button to stop the blender. Serve in individual cups.

What Your Child Is Learning

By learning to follow simple recipes like this one, you are teaching your child more than how to follow directions. Making a banana shake shows him how a blender works and he sees firsthand how foods change when they are combined. New taste combinations expand his palate while healthy combinations of foods like fruit shakes reinforce good nutritional habits.

More Things to Do   Try this recipe with strawberries, either fresh or frozen. You'll need about a dozen medium-sized fresh strawberries. If you're using frozen berries, use about 1½ cups. Add 1 teaspoon of sugar to the strawberry mixture.

Ages two and up: Create a frozen banana treat! Peel a banana and insert a Popsicle stick into one end of it. Place in a zip-seal bag or wrap it in aluminum foil and put it in the freezer. Enjoy when frozen.

English Muffin Pizzas

▶ **AGES:**
2 years to 4+ years

▶ **ACTIVITY TIME:**
20 to 30 minutes

Ingredients and Supplies

- ◆ an English muffin
- ◆ spaghetti sauce
- ◆ grated cheese (mozzarella is best)
- ◆ small plastic measuring cup
- ◆ a blunt knife
- ◆ a baking sheet or tinfoil
- ◆ salt and pepper to taste

(1) SPLIT MUFFIN, SPREAD SAUCE

Recipe

Split the English muffin in half with a fork. Give your child a small measuring cup with some spaghetti sauce in it. About ¼ of a cup will do. He can pour the sauce onto both halves of the muffin. Spread the sauce evenly with a knife.

Sprinkle with grated cheese. Add salt and pepper to taste. Place on a baking sheet or a piece of tinfoil. Bake in a toaster oven or conventional oven at 350° for between five and ten minutes, until the cheese is completely melted.

Enjoy!

(2) ADD CHEESE, SALT, PEPPER

What Your Child Is Learning

It is rare that a child is able to prepare his own main dish for a meal. Making his own pizza using a recipe with only a few simple steps will give him that wonderful feeling of "I can do it!" Perfect for that stage when they want to do things all by themselves, this recipe also teaches your child about sequencing and following directions. Do you put the cheese on before or after the sauce? Let's read the directions.

More Things to Do

Make peanut butter and jelly sandwiches together. Use cookie cutters to cut the sandwich into exciting shapes!

Have a special Sunday breakfast! Write with pancake batter in the skillet. Make a personalized pancake shaped like the first letter in your child's name!

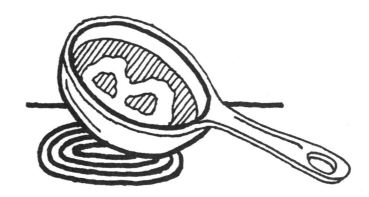

Snap! Instant Pudding

► AGES:
18 months to 4+ years

► ACTIVITY TIME:
5 minutes

Ingredients and Supplies

♦ store-bought instant pudding
♦ milk
♦ a measuring cup
♦ a large heavy-duty storage bag with a zip-seal closure
♦ a spoon

Recipe

Pour contents of the pudding package into the zip-seal bag. Measure the milk as called for on the package. Add the milk to the zip-seal bag. Make sure that the seal is completely closed.

Your child is now free to shake the bag. As she shakes the bag, the ingredients are mixed and the pudding will form. When the ingredients are thoroughly mixed, the pudding is ready to be eaten. If you like, refrigerate it for about five minutes before serving.

The pudding can be squeezed or spooned from the bag into a bowl for serving.

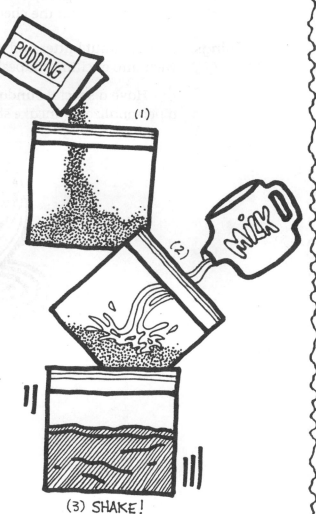

(1)

(2)

(3) SHAKE!

| **What Your Child Is Learning** | When two different foods are combined, changes can occur, even if heat or cooling are not involved. The zip-seal bag lets your child watch what is happening. Making this recipe is such fun it is a game in itself. |

More Things to Do   Try new flavors! Pudding can also be made in a Tupperware container. It's easy to shake and there is no risk of spilling.

Make some Jell-O! It's so funny how it wiggles.

Make Your Own Ice Cream

▶ AGES:	▶ ACTIVITY TIME:
2 years (with some help) to 4+ years	**1 hour to 1 hour and 30 minutes**

Recipe #1
(feeds 4)

Ingredients and Supplies

+ 1 pint of heavy cream
+ ½ cup of sugar
+ 1½ teaspoons of vanilla
+ lots of ice, at least one large bag
+ salt—kosher is best because of the size of the grains
+ 1–2 coffee cans with lids (sand down the rough edges first with sandpaper)
+ 1–2 large plastic buckets
+ large mixing bowl
+ a cake spatula, spoon, or blunt knife

Recipe

Mix the cream, sugar, and vanilla in a mixing bowl. Pour the mixture, dividing it evenly among the coffee cans. Make sure that the lids are on tight.

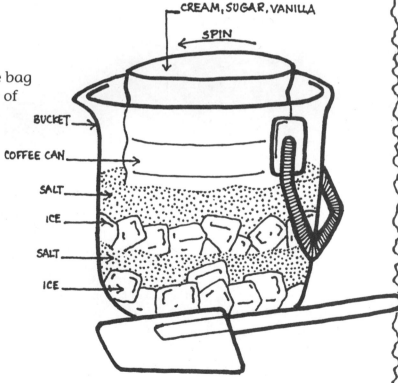

CREAM, SUGAR, VANILLA
SPIN
BUCKET
COFFEE CAN
SALT
ICE
SALT
ICE

Prepare a "freezer" for the ice cream in a bucket. Line the bottom of each bucket with a thick layer of ice. Sprinkle a generous layer of salt on top of the ice. Place the cans into the buckets. Continue to layer around each can with ice and salt until only the top of the can is showing.

Take turns "spinning" the cans around inside of the bucket. It is best to have a group of people to help you. Turning the can is important because the spinning motion keeps the mixture from forming big ice crystals and assures that the whole mixture will freeze around the same time.

Check the ice cream in the can periodically. The sides will freeze first, leaving the middle soupy. Scrape the ice cream off of the sides with a cake spatula or spoon to help it freeze more evenly. Do this two or three times in the course of the freezing.

The ice cream takes between thirty to sixty minutes to freeze completely. Cans that are less full will freeze more quickly. If you double the recipe, double the number of cans and buckets you are using.

Version #2 The main benefit of this variation is that young kids have more to do while they are waiting for the ice cream to be ready. Also, because the portions in the cans are smaller, the ice cream in this version freezes much faster.

Ingredients and Supplies
- same ingredients as the above ice cream mixture
- small tin cans like clean tuna fish or cat food cans with lids (lids to fit cat food cans are sold at the supermarket), one for each person
- coffee cans with lids, one for each person

Directions Mix the recipe according to the directions for Version #1. Pour the mixture into the small cans. Replace the lids.

Next, layer ice and salt in the bottom of each coffee can. Place the small can with the mixture inside the coffee can. Fill the remainder of the can with successive layers of ice and salt. When the coffee can is full, replace the lid.

This is where the fun really begins. Sit with your child in an open space on the floor. Take turns rolling the coffee cans full of ice cream back and forth between the two of you. Rolling the can is the same spinning action involved in turning a can in a large bucket of ice.

This mixture should freeze in about ten to fifteen minutes.

What Your Child Is Learning

Is there really ice in ice cream? How do things freeze? Making ice cream is a treat for your taste buds and a great family activity that gets everyone involved. Measuring the ingredients, preparing the "freezer" buckets, and watching as the ingredients change form is a process that is rich with learning opportunities. Your child can help you to measure, pour, layer the ice and salt, spin the can, and test to see how the ice cream is progressing.

More Things to Do

Flavor your ice cream with fresh fruits, various extracts, or chocolate chips. With Version #2, each member of the family can customize their own flavor. Don't forget to write down your recipes!

Note: Do not use chocolate syrup as a flavoring ingredient for this recipe. When syrup is added, the mixture will not freeze properly. Instead, use chocolate extract or chocolate chips for flavor.

▶ *Why do you need salt in the bucket of ice?*

As ice melts, it absorbs heat. When salt is present, it helps the ice to melt faster, allowing the ice to absorb the heat from the ice cream mixture more quickly than it would if salt were not present.

▶ This recipe is made for kids because the measurements do not need to be very precise for the ice cream to come out tasting delicious!

Perfect Popsicles

▶ **AGES:**
18 months to 4+ years

▶ **ACTIVITY TIME:**
5 to 10 minutes

Ingredients and Supplies

- ◆ juice of any kind: orange, pineapple, grape, apple or lemonade
- ◆ ice cube trays, one tray for each flavor of juice
- ◆ a small plastic measuring cup
- ◆ an eyedropper or a Dixie cup
- ◆ Popsicle (craft) sticks

Recipe

Pour some juice into a small measuring cup. If you have an eyedropper, show your child how to use the dropper to fill the empty compartments of the ice cube tray. A Dixie cup with a crease put in it will work too for pouring.

Once the compartments are filled, insert a Popsicle stick in each one. The sticks don't have to stand up straight for the Popsicles to work.

Place the full trays in the freezer overnight. When frozen, twist the tray to release the Popsicles.

Sit in a cool place, eat your Popsicles, and relax together.

What Your Child Is Learning

This recipe shows your child that freezing food changes its consistency. Also, this is an opportunity to talk about what different flavors taste like and to try different combinations of fruit juices. What is his favorite juice? What is his favorite food? Do the two of you like the same foods? Is there anything that either of you don't like to eat?

More Things to Do

Combine fruit juices and taste-test them. If you like the combination, turn the juice into Popsicles!

Make homemade lemonade. Squeeze the juice of one lemon and add 1 to 2 teaspoons of sugar to taste for each glass. Pour lemonade over lots of ice.

No-Bake Cookies

▶ AGES:	▶ ACTIVITY TIME:
2 to 4+ years	15 to 20 minutes

(1) PEANUT BUTTER + WATER

Ingredients and Supplies

+ ½ cup of peanut butter
+ 2 cups of powdered milk
+ ¼ cup honey*
+ a measuring cup
+ a large mixing bowl
+ a wooden spoon
+ teaspoons
+ shredded coconut, chocolate chips (optional)

(2) MIX INGREDIENTS

Recipe

Show older children how peanut butter can be measured with a measuring cup and some water. Fill a measuring cup with ½ cup of water. Point out the water line to your child. You can use a laundry pencil or piece of masking tape to make a mark at the water line. Now, add peanut butter until the water line is at 1 cup. Together, look at the change in the water line.

(3) ROLL BALLS INTO COCONUT AND CHOCOLATE CHIPS

*Honey is recommended for children over one year only. For information, see "Snack Collage," p. 194.

Pour out the water. Add the peanut butter to the mixing bowl. Combine the peanut butter with the milk and honey. Mix them together well.

With a teaspoon, scoop up some batter and roll it into a ball. If you like, roll the balls in chocolate chips or shredded coconut. The cookies are ready to serve.

What Your Child Is Learning

This is an experience in measuring and combining a few simple foods to create a new taste sensation.

More Things to Do

Use this recipe as an edible version of play dough. With this dough, she can play with cookie cutters, rolling pins, and plastic knives. When she's done, she can eat all of her creations.

See our recipe for "Peanut Butter" on p. 188.

CHAPTER 9

"How To" for Parents

How to Make a Paste and Paint Brush

▶ **FOR AGES:**
12 months to 4+ years

▶ **TIME:**
5 minutes

Materials
- a small piece of sponge, about 1½ inches
- a Popsicle (craft) stick—available at art and craft stores
- a rubber band

Directions   Wrap the piece of sponge around one end of the stick, bending it so that the end of the stick is covered with the foam. Secure the sponge with a rubber band.

This economical, replaceable brush is perfect for pasting and gluing, and it can also be used for painting.

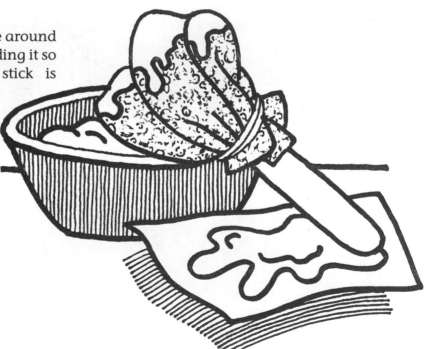

How to Make a "No-Spill" Paint Container

▶ **FOR AGES:**
12 months to 4+ years

▶ **TIME:**
5 minutes

Materials
- a small plastic Tupperware container or a clear plastic supermarket container with a tight-fitting lid (the heavy kind used for deli salads and grated cheeses)
- a utility knife or scissors
- aluminum foil

Directions

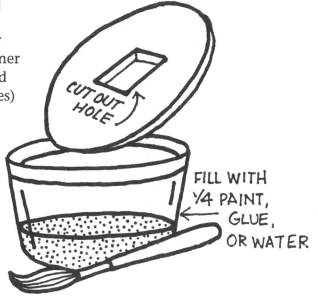

CUT OUT HOLE

FILL WITH ¼ PAINT, GLUE, OR WATER

The idea behind a paint container is that paint or glue can be stored in it and the container will hold most of the paint (or glue) in the event of a spill. The keys here are that the bottom of the container be stable and the opening in the top just large enough for a brush to fit through.

These containers work best for short-handled brushes. Brushes with long handles tend to tip the container over. Styrofoam trays (such as the ones that come with meats from the supermarket) should be used with longer brushes. With a brush or a spoon, apply a thin layer of paint to the tray and use the tray as a palette. If the tray happens to flip over, there will not be enough paint in it to make a big mess.

To make your container, take the utility knife or scissors and cut a small square out of the middle of the container lid, just big enough for a paintbrush. Replace the lid.

Before you use it, fill a quarter of the container with paint. This will help to weight the bottom so that it won't tip. Between painting sessions, the hole in the lid can be plugged with a ball of aluminum foil to keep the paint moist for storage. Plan to store tempera paint for about two weeks with this type of container.

If you open the paint container after storing and find that the paint has dried up, reconstitute it by adding a little bit of water.

These containers can be used for all projects calling for tempera paints and can also be filled with water or white glue.

Children's nonspill paint pots are available, often in sets of four or six, from art supply, toy, and educational supply stores.

How to Make Round Crayons

▶ **FOR AGES:**
18 months to 4+ years

▶ **TIME:**
45 minutes

Materials

- ◆ small pieces of crayon, preferably leftover chunks or crayon shavings
- ◆ a muffin tin (preferably nonstick)
- ◆ shallow pan filled with 1 inch of water
- ◆ oven, preheated to 300°
- ◆ pot holders
- ◆ foil muffin cups (optional)

Directions

Remove any paper wrappers from the crayons and sort crayons by color. Older children can help you with the sorting but may not be able to remove the wrappers.

Place the crayon pieces in the muffin tin compartments. If you use foil muffin cups, they will give you "ridges" on the edges of your crayon. You can choose to make a solid-colored crayon, using scraps of a single color, for example, all greens. To make a multicolored crayon, include many different colored bits in each compartment.

Each tin should have either all solid or all multicolored crayons, because the time spent in the oven is different for each one.

Preheat the oven to 350°. Place the muffin tin in a pan with ½ inch of water in the bottom. Place it in the oven. Leave the oven light on and begin to check the oven after about five minutes so that the two of you can watch the melting process.

For solid colors, heat for ten to fifteen minutes. Remove your new crayons from the oven when the wax has melted. For multicolored crayons, take the tray out of the oven as soon as the pieces start to melt. If they get too soft, the colors will mix and the wax will turn brown.

Allow the crayons to cool. How long does it take for the wax to harden? Place the muffin tin in a pan of ice water to speed up the process. When the wax has cooled, score around the crayons with a blunt knife. Your crayons will pop right out of the muffin tin.

Note: We don't suggest using a microwave because the wax gets too hot too fast and doesn't melt evenly. We have had better results with a conventional oven.

How to Dye Pasta

▶ FOR AGES:
2 to 4+ years

▶ TIME:
10 to 15 minutes

Materials

- large tube pasta like ziti or rigatoni, about half a box per color
- food coloring
- a large bowl
- water
- cookie sheets or a plastic tray
- waxed paper
- a spoon or rubber gloves

(1) ADD WATER AND COLORING TO BOWL

(2) ADD PASTA TO BOWL

(3) MIX PASTA

(4) SPREAD TO DRY

Directions

Fill a bowl with ¼ cup of water. Add 20 drops of food coloring to the water for lighter colors, 25 to 30 drops of coloring for darker colors. You can combine two colors, using 10 drops of green and 10 drops of blue for blue-green, red and blue to make purple, or green and yellow to make light green.

Add the pasta to the bowl of water, between one third and one half of the total box. With a spoon or rubber gloves, roll the pasta in the food coloring and water mixture so that it is com-

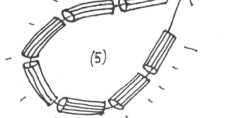

(5)

pletely coated with dye. The pasta will start to soften when it comes in contact with water. As soon as the pasta is saturated with color, remove it from the bowl and spread it out to dry on a tray covered with waxed paper.

Finished pasta can be used to string a necklace or make collages.

More Things to Do

Substitute alcohol for the water in this recipe. It makes the colors brighter.

Dye pasta with powdered tempera paint. There are some wonderful colors available, like turquoise, silver, and gold. A good ratio to use is 3 to 4 tablespoons to $1/4$ cup water.

See instructions for "Stringing Beads" (p. 25) and "Crazy Collages" (p. 29).

How to Make Easy Potato Stamps

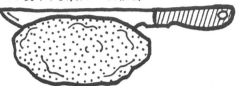

(1) CUT POTATO IN HALF

▶ FOR AGES:
18 months to 4+ years

▶ TIME:
10 minutes per stamp

Materials

- ♦ 2 or 3 medium to large potatoes (each potato makes 2 stamps)
- ♦ cookie cutters in different shapes and sizes
- ♦ a paring knife

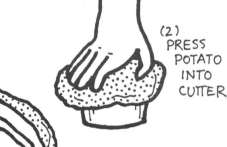

(2) PRESS POTATO INTO CUTTER

Directions

Hold a potato lengthwise and cut it in half across the middle, so that the halves are large enough for your child to hold on to easily.

(3) TRIM AWAY EXCESS

Next, ask your child to choose a cookie cutter. Place it on a flat surface with the cutting edge facing up. Place the potato on top of the cutter, with the fleshy side down. Line up the edge so that the outline of the cutter is under-

(4) PRESS POTATO TO INKPAD, THEN TO PAPER

neath the potato. Press down firmly on the potato so that the cookie cutter makes an incision about $1/8$ inch deep.

With the cookie cutter embedded in the potato, carefully trim around the outline of the incised shape with your knife. Slowly shave away the excess, leaving the cut outline raised. You only need to remove a thin layer of the excess around the design for the stamp to work. The cookie cutter will make it easy to trim without slicing the design by mistake. If it is difficult to trim around the cutter, you may remove it.

Try out your new stamp with an ink pad. To learn more ways to use your new stamp and more ideas for printing projects, follow directions for "Printing with Fruits and Vegetables."

More Things to Do Make another stamp, this time of your own design. Carve the potato freehand, using your paring knife. You may find it helpful to sketch out ideas for your design first on a piece of paper.

See instructions for "Sponge Printing" (p. 40) and "Printing with String" (p. 44).

See instructions for "Printing with Fruits and Vegetables," p. 42.

How to Make an Ocean in a Bottle

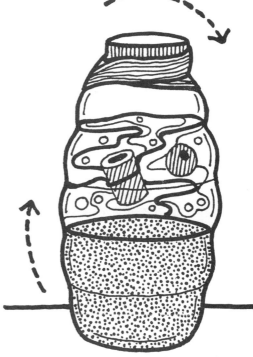

▶ FOR AGES:	▶ TIME:
Infant to 4+ years	**10 to 15 minutes**

Materials

For infants
- small clear plastic soda bottles with lids (single-serving size), washed and with the labels removed
- colorful plastic beads, sequins, bits of confetti or Mylar

For toddlers and preschoolers
- either small or 1- or 2-liter clear plastic soda bottles
- mineral oil (baby oil)
- water
- food coloring
- duct tape

Directions

Fill the soda bottle one third to one half full with water. Add drops of food coloring to the water until you reach the desired color. You can use any color you like—blue and green dyes combined make the traditional "ocean" color.

Fill the remainder of the bottle with mineral oil, leaving 2½ to 3 inches of air at the top. This is necessary to simulate the rolling of waves. For infants in particular, also include in the bottle some colorful objects like plastic be ls or bits of Mylar for them to focus on. Screw the lid on tightly and secure it with .eavy duct tape.

Please note: Because of possible leakage and small items included in the design of this toy, adult supervision is necessary when it's in use.

What Your Child Is Learning

Infants are attracted to shiny objects and bright colors and will enjoy watching bits of colorful material floating inside the bottle. Older children will like the action of the "waves." Preschoolers are a bit young for the science lesson behind the toy, but it is still great fun. The biggest lesson learned from this activity is probably that not all good toys have to come from the store—the two of you can make them together!

▶ *How does it work?*

The principle behind the "ocean" is that mineral oil and water will not mix. The movement of the two separate liquids within the bottle gives the illusion of waves.

How to Make Sewing Cards

Materials

- ◆ tagboard (file folder material) or lightweight cardboard
- ◆ a pencil
- ◆ large-sized stencils (optional) (available at craft and educational supply stores)
- ◆ scissors
- ◆ a hole punch
- ◆ long shoelaces, plastic lacing, or nylon cording
- ◆ masking tape (if you use cording)

Directions

Trace some shapes on the tagboard. These can be simple geometric shapes like triangles, circles, and squares. You can also make some simple animal shapes, freehand or with stencils. For younger children who are sewing for the first time, keep your shapes large, around 6 to 8 inches across so that they are easy to handle.

With scissors, cut out the shapes you have drawn. Draw a

line around the outline of the shape, inset ½ inch from the edge. Using this line as your guide, make holes with the hole punch along the outline of the shape. The holes should be about ½ inch apart.

Cut a piece of cord or use a lace long enough to sew all the way around the card. If you are using nylon cording or plastic lacing, wrap a piece of tape around one end of the cord, so that the tape comes to a point like a needle. This will help your child to sew.

Tie a double knot in the remaining end of the lace, and pull it through the card. Your child is now ready to begin sewing.

Activity

Show him how to begin by weaving the lace up through the first hole, then across and down into the next one. Next, weave across the back of the card and up through the next hole. Continue all the way around the card.

What Your Child Is Learning

Through the simple weaving motion involved in this activity, your child will learn many skills, including eye-hand coordination, small motor skills, manual dexterity, concentration, and patience.

How to Make Dave's Helicopter

► FOR AGES: **18 months to 4+ years**   ► TIME: **10 minutes**

Materials

- a piece of paper: an old calendar page or heavy paper is best, but any kind will do
- a pencil
- a ruler
- scissors

Directions

1. Measure and cut a piece of paper into a rectangle 3 by 9 inches.
2. Make a mark with a pencil in the center of one of the 3-inch sides. Draw a line starting at the pencil point, going down the center of the paper lengthwise. The line should go about a third of the length of the paper. Cut along the line to make a long slit.
3. Mark two lines on each long side, at right angles to where the slit ends in the center of the paper. The lines should stop 1/4 to 1/2 inch before the center of the paper. Cut along the two lines with scissors. Do not cut off the paper rectangles.
4. Fold the long, uncut portion of the paper into thirds, as you would fold a

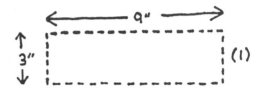

piece of paper to put it in an envelope. The paper sides will overlap each other. This will make a "stem."

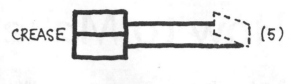

5. Make a ½-inch crease along the bottom of the stem. Fold back along the crease to make a folded flap.

6. Hold the paper vertically, by the folded stem. The two pieces of paper on the top form two rectangles. These are the "chopper blades." Arrange these rectangles so that each faces a different direction in a zigzag shape.

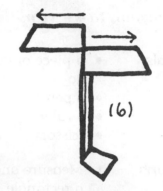

7. Your helicopter is now ready to fly. Stand on a chair, let go, and watch it swirl!

Activity

Cut and fold a piece of paper to the specifications in the diagram. Stand on a chair and drop the helicopter. Watch it spiral to the ground. An old calendar page or drawing will make a pattern as it spirals.

What Your Child Is Learning

This playful activity is entertaining for both grown-ups and kids. The lesson involved is a good one. With a little ingenuity, even a material as simple as a piece of paper can be cut and manipulated into a fairly sophisticated toy.

How to Make a Box House

Materials

- a large cardboard box
- a wide-tipped marker
- a utility knife
- clear packing tape, duct tape, or masking tape
- a yardstick (optional)
- decorating materials (optional) like: contact paper, stickers, wallpaper, tissue paper, magazine cuttings (and paste), tempera paint

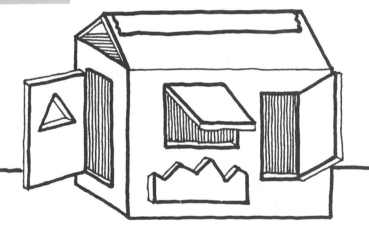

Directions

Tape the bottom of the box closed so that the seams are reinforced.

Your child can help you decide what the house will look like. With the marker, draw out where the door and windows will

be. Large, simple shapes like squares, circles, and rectangles work best. Plan to have one or two shapes per side. A yardstick may help you draw straight lines.

Once the lines are drawn, cut out the windows and door, using the knife. You may need to go over the cardboard twice, once to score it and another time to remove the shape.

Doors can be "hinged" by scoring the cardboard with the knife, and cutting only halfway through the thickness of the board. For a doorknob, cut a round hole big enough for your child to loop his finger through, so that he can pull the door open and closed.

For a pointed roof, unfold the flaps on the top of the box. Angle the two larger pieces toward each other so that they meet to make a pointed roof. Tape them loosely into place.

If the two pieces don't meet in the middle, add an extra strip of cardboard to the top to bridge the gap between the two sides. Bend the two smaller flaps up to meet the angle of the roof. Trace the outline of the slope on the cardboard flaps to create the front and back sides of the house, where the roof joins. Cut the outline with a knife.

Secure the roof and sides with tape. Clear packing tape is preferred—it is invisible and also harder to remove if you have a child who loves to take things apart.

Collect props to use in the house, like plastic plates, dishes or glasses, a feather duster, and dress-up clothes. Put up wallpaper inside the house. Get a carpet remnant for the floor. The more details, the better.

▶ "I brought home a large box for my two-year-old and we colored the outside with markers. She loves to sit inside it and look out the opening. Now that the outside is decorated, we're working on the inside. Who would have thought she would get so many hours of entertainment from such an inexpensive toy?"

What Your Child Is Learning

Providing your child with a setting for pretend play helps to make play more "real." Imagination is more vivid when children can project ideas onto a three-dimensional set, such as a house, a grocery store, or a school bus, that contains elements that the child is familiar with.

More Things to Do

Decorate the house with your child! Use materials like stickers, markers, shiny paper, tissue, wallpaper scraps, or magazine cuttings. The house can be painted with tempera paints. Before painting or pasting, lay the whole structure on newspaper or a large piece of plastic.

Make other cardboard creations! Make a school bus out of a long box; a store or a school out of big square boxes.

> ▶ *Where can I get a really large box?*
>
> Call local appliance stores or toy stores; often they will save one for you if you ask.

How to Make a
Homemade Puppet

Materials

- a sock
- a needle and thread (with colored thread the stitching becomes part of the design)
- any or all of the following: felt or fabric scraps, buttons, yarn or ribbons, pom-poms, etc.
- scissors

Directions

Place the sock on your hand. You can place your thumb in the heel of the sock and your four fingers in the toe area so that when you move your fingers, the puppet's mouth will open and close.

You can plan a puppet with a specific character in mind or just choose the decorations as you go along. If you are designing the puppet as you go, start with a prominent feature, like eyes or hair. Once the first feature is in place, it is usually easier to think about what comes next. How would eyebrows look with these eyes? In this way, each decision will contribute to the final look of the puppet.

If you have a specific idea in mind, it is helpful to think of key features that you want to be sure to include. For example, a mouse puppet would not be complete without large ears, whiskers, and a long tail.

Color choices can help to create a realistic or whimsical feeling. Lots of brightly colored threads, patterned fabric scraps, and ribbons could combine to create a make-believe kitten, while a black sock with white felt and green button eyes could look just like your real kitten.

Be sure to sew on buttons and other items tightly, so that they can't be pulled off easily. Always supervise small children closely when playing with a homemade toy.

What Your Child Is Learning

A homemade puppet is one of the first toys that will catch the attention of an infant and engage him in eye contact. Puppets maintain a child's interest throughout her growing years, because of their ability to adapt to different personalities and scenarios. A puppet is a multidimensional toy, limited only by your imagination.

More Things to Do

Younger children may enjoy playing a game that teaches the different body parts. The puppet can ask the child to point to the puppet's nose. Can your child point to the puppet's nose? What about her nose? Can she point to her eyes? Her teeth? . . .

Let the puppet tell your child a story about "Long ago and far away . . ."

Build a puppet theater and put on a play! See instructions for "How to Make a Puppet Theater," which follow.

> ▶ Puppets are wonderful toys and they are even more special when a parent has made one. Even an infant will respond to a puppet, because the features strongly resemble a person's face.

How to Make a Puppet Theater

▶ FOR AGES:	▶ TIME:
2 to 4+ years	45 minutes

Materials
- a large cardboard box
- utility knife
- a wide-tipped marker
- clear packing tape, duct tape, or masking tape
- a yardstick (optional)
- decorating materials (optional) like contact paper (shelf paper), wallpaper, and colored tissue with glue or paint

Directions
Reinforce the bottom of the box with tape, so that it is stable. Remove the top flaps on the box with the knife, so that the top is completely open.

With the box upright, draw an outline of a door on one of the smaller sides. A yardstick may help you to draw straight lines. When you are designing the door, leave about 5 inches or more of space around the top and sides of the door to keep the box stable. The bottom of the door will be cut all the way down to the floor.

Remove the door with the knife. You may have to go over the cardboard twice, once to score it and another time to cut it away completely. For older kids, you might want to "hinge" the door instead of removing it completely.

To make a hinge, cut only halfway through the thickness of the cardboard with your knife. Then, bend the door so that it will swing open and closed as if it were on hinges. Cut a round hole where the doorknob would be, big enough for your child to loop his finger through so he can open and close the door.

Draw a rectangle on one of the long sides of the box. This will be the stage where "plays" will take place. The rectangle should begin about halfway up the side of the box. Again, leave a border of 5 inches or more around the sides and top of the rectangle. Remove the shape with your knife.

Decorate the box together. Contact paper is easy to use and covers large areas quickly. Wallpaper, tissue and glue, paint, and markers are some other options. If you are decorating with paint or glue, place newspaper or a sheet of plastic underneath the box before you begin. (For tips on how to decorate your box, see "Crazy Collages," p. 29.)

Once the box has been decorated, draw a picture to use as a "setting" for a play. The drawing could be of the inside of a store, a classroom, or the countryside. Tape it to the back wall of the box, so that it can be seen through the window. Change the setting periodically to keep your child interested.

What Your Child Is Learning

Giving your child a stage on which to put on plays adds that extra something that makes playing more special. Making a puppet theater for your child is an affirmation of your child's imagination and creativity.

More Things to Do

Make your own puppet! It's a great toy for infants and older kids. See "How to Make a Homemade Puppet" (p. 228), "Shadow Shows" (p. 185), and "Paper Bag Puppets," p. 140.

How to Make a "This Is Me" Book

▶ FOR AGES:	▶ TIME:
12 months to 4+ years	*1 to 2 hours*

Materials

- ◆ a small photo album with peel-back pages
- ◆ 6 to 8 pictures of: family members, your home, your child's bedroom, pets, pictures of your child
- ◆ any handmade projects or drawings that you have saved or that your child has completed recently
- ◆ tracings of your child's hands and feet
- ◆ magazine pictures of objects that have meaning to your child
- ◆ a small hand mirror (optional)
- ◆ heavy paper and masking tape, to make a pocket for a cassette tape (optional)

Directions

For infants and young children who can be hard on books, photo albums with peel-back pages are a practical and sturdy choice. They do not tear easily, and you can start with five or six pages, adding more as you go along.

Pictures, drawings, and tracings can easily be arranged and rearranged within these pages. Ideas to include could be favorite toys, activities, foods, places, friends, and outfits. The title of the book will be *This Is Me*.

Each page should include one or two items—a photograph, magazine cut-out, or picture of something that is important to your child. For example, this is Alex at one year old. He loves the swing. His favorite food is Cheerios. This is his uncle Peter, who loves to kiss him.

You can use this book as an introduction to reading by "naming" together the items in the book. Make movable labels using strips of paper and a marker. Be sure to print clearly.

You might want to include a cassette tape of your child's voice. To make a pouch for a cassette, cut a piece of heavy paper to size, 6 by $3^{1}/_{2}$ inches. Attach the paper to the page of the book by taping the bottom and two sides. Leave the top open for the tape to slide in.

Another idea is to adhere a small mirror to one of the pages with duct tape or packing tape. Your child will enjoy looking into it.

What Your Child Is Learning

Making a book all about your child builds pride and enhances self-esteem. Through looking at pictures and talking about what is in the book, she gains a sense of her own uniqueness. A book like this makes a wonderful discussion tool while your child is young and a treasured memento from childhood when she has grown.

▶ *What else can I do to keep a record of my child's growth?*

Start a collection! In Playspace, we have on display a collection of shoes that belonged to one little girl from the time she was a year old until she was twelve. She's in college now, but visitors still stop to comment about the shoes on the wall.

How to Make a Portfolio for Your Child's Artwork

Materials

- 2 pieces of stiff cardboard, 12 by 18 inches
- masking tape or duct tape
- a piece of ribbon or heavy yarn, 48 inches long
- a stapler
- decorating materials (optional): crayons, markers, shelf paper, rubber stamps and a stamp pad, fabric or wallpaper, and white glue or glue sticks

Directions

Lay the pieces of cardboard next to each other (with the pieces touching), along the 18-inch sides. Next, tape the two sides together along the seam between the two pieces. Allow a small gap of about ⅛ inch between the two pieces. Apply pieces of tape to the full length of the cardboard.

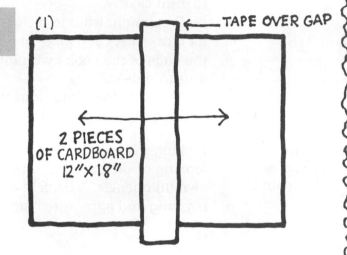

(1) TAPE OVER GAP

2 PIECES OF CARDBOARD 12" × 18"

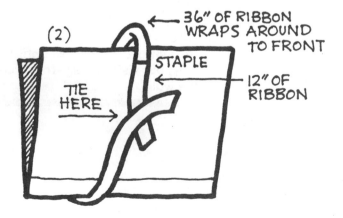

(2) 36" OF RIBBON WRAPS AROUND TO FRONT

STAPLE

TIE HERE

12" OF RIBBON

Flip the pieces over and apply tape to the other side of the seam. The tape will form an effective hinge so that the portfolio can open and close.

The portfolio may be decorated with a variety of materials. Rubber stamps or markers can be used to design a lively cover. Shelf paper, wallpaper, or fabric can be cut to 12 by 18 inches and attached to the cardboard for a more finished look. Wallpaper or fabric must be attached with glue.

When the decorating is finished, staple the ribbon to the cardboard for use as a closure. Attach the ribbon to the open end, opposite the taped seam. Staple the ribbon in the center of one piece, inset 2 inches from the edge. To attach the ribbon properly, staple the ribbon asymmetrically, leaving 12 inches of ribbon on one side of the staple and 36 inches of ribbon on the other.

Once artwork is inside, close the portfolio by wrapping the long piece of ribbon around the portfolio once, meeting the shorter piece to make a bow.

AFTERWORD

One of the most fascinating things about toddlers and preschoolers is that they already possess such distinct personalities. Each child's learning style is unique. In each of these activities, from playing with blocks to washing babies, you can actually see your child making connections for the first time, moving through a sequence of steps, each step leading to the next. Children's individuality and creativity show in how they choose to move from one point to another. It's fun to watch and be a part of this process.

Has your child done anything that has surprised you? What changes or growth have you seen in your child from her first activity until now? Which types of activities have held her interest? Is she inclined to be more verbal or more physical? Do you see any of your own personality traits in your child?

It is easy to notice small changes in your child, but it may be much harder to see your growth as a parent. The parent-child relationship is always evolving and changing. It is a dynamic relationship; the challenges you both face continue to change as your child grows. Give yourself time to reflect on these changes and to appreciate what you have accomplished.

Did you surprise yourself? Did you learn anything new? What do you feel were your successes? What would you do differently next time? As time went on, did you grow more comfortable with your own skills and abilities? Has this experience made you more aware of your parenting style?

We hope, through this book, to instill in parents greater confidence in themselves and the quality of the learning experiences they are able to provide for their children. Our parenting strategies highlight communication between the parent and child, with an emphasis on understanding and fostering your child's interests and motivations. This style of interaction and the associated communication skills can carry over from these activities into other areas of your lives, enriching them with understanding and mutual respect.

We hope that you will get years of enjoyment from these activities. And if you are ever in Boston, come and visit us in Playspace at The Children's Museum.

APPENDIX

Where to Buy Supplies

Save at Home

calendars (old)
cardboard boxes
cards
clothes and accessories for dress-up
coffee cans
egg cartons
juice cans (sand sharp edges with sandpaper)
magazines
newspapers

paper towel rolls
ribbons and bows
shoe boxes
squeeze bottles from syrup or dishwashing liquid
Styrofoam grocery trays
toilet paper rolls
wrapping paper
yogurt containers with lids

From the Supermarket

aluminum foil
aluminum pans (disposable)
baster
bleach (for cleaning)
coffee filters
cookie cutters
cooking oil

dishwashing liquid
Dixie cups
dried beans
flour
foil muffin cups
food coloring*
Ivory Snow Flakes

Tip: Food coloring can also be purchased from a baker's supply store. The dye is more concentrated, the bottles are bigger, and there is a larger color selection. Ask your local baker or check the yellow pages for companies in your area.

lunch bags
muffin tin
paper plates
pasta
pie tins (disposable)
rice

rolling pin
salt
shoelaces
sponges
straws
zip-seal bags

From the Hardware Store

automotive hand cleaner (will remove crayon marks
    from walls or furniture)
bucket
cellophane tape
clear contact paper (shelf paper)
clothespins and clothesline (to hang up artwork
    while it dries)
dishwashing tub (for water play)
duct tape
foam brushes in various sizes
funnels

gardening stakes
kitty litter box (for rice play)
masking tape
painter's tarp (plastic, at least 2 mil. thickness)
rubber bands
sandpaper
scissors (adult)
shower curtain (to protect the floor)
sponges
string
thumbtacks

From the Art Supply or Craft Store

chalk
colored cellophane
construction paper
craft (Popsicle) sticks
crayons
Cray-Pas
doilies
fabric paints (designed specifically for painting on
    T-shirts or other fabrics)
feathers
felt

finger paint
finger paint paper
glitter
glue
glue sticks (for ages three and up)
manila paper
mural paper (in rolls)
Mylar
paintbrushes
paint containers with no-spill lids
paper (white)

poster board
print-making roller
push pins (like thumbtacks, to display artwork)
ribbons
scissors (children's)
sequins
smock
stamps
stamp pads (check label for washable ink)
stapler

string
tagboard
tempera paints (poster paint)
tissue paper (comes in single color or assorted
    packages)
tulle (decorative netting)
utility knife
watercolor sets
water-soluble markers
yarn

Tip: Educational supply stores also carry many of these items, which can be easily ordered through a catalog. For a list of companies in your area, check the yellow pages or your local library. However, keep in mind that you pay for the convenience of ordering by phone through additional shipping costs.

From the Toy or Educational Supply Store

blocks (wood)
Duplo blocks
finger paints
finger paint paper
Lincoln Logs
mural paper (in rolls)
peg sorters
play settings: farms, houses, garages, etc., with
    people and animals
pop beads

puzzles
rolling pin (child-sized)
shape sorters
smocks
squeeze bottles with caps (for glue or paint)
stacking rings
Star builders
stencils
Tinker Toys

From the Office Supply Store

brass fasteners (for shadow puppets and ornaments)
cellophane tape
envelopes
file folders (good, inexpensive heavy paper. Cut them
    in half.)

file labels (make great stickers. Use round ones in
    assorted colors.)
hole punch
markers
masking tape

paper clips
pens
stamps

stapler
storage boxes
Xerox paper (for drawing)

From the Discount Supply Store (like Walmart or Woolworth) or 99¢ Store

artificial flowers
baskets (for loose materials)
costume jewelry

place mats (plastic)
plastic tub with a lid for storage
shower curtain (to protect the floor)

From the Fabric Store

buttons
fabric
felt (look for bags of remnants)

ribbons
wiggly eyes

From Wholesale Clubs

Most clubs require some type of membership fee. Buying in bulk may not be practical for everyone, but for people with more than one child or a play group or parties to host, it can be a good option. While you're there check out the selection of children's books.

colored chalk
colored construction paper
crayons
dried beans
lunch bags
markers
paper plates
pasta
pencils

plastic food storage containers with lids (can be purchased there for storing paint and other supplies)
rice
scissors
Styrofoam trays (use as a paint tray, and many other uses)
Xerox paper (great for drawing)

From Yard Sales or Secondhand Stores

accessories for dress-up:
belts
costume jewelry
dresses
handbags

hats
shoes
sport coats
suitcase

From the Appliance Store or Shoe Store

cardboard boxes (free, call ahead of time, and bring
a shopping bag with you to carry home empty
shoe boxes)

From the Carpet Store

samples of discontinued carpeting (free, call ahead
of time)

From the Wallpaper Store

sample books of discontinued wallpaper (free, call
ahead of time)

From the Fish Market

whole fish (for Fish Prints)

Making Adjustments:
Tailoring Activities to Fit Your Child's Age and Abilities

My child is younger than the age guidelines you suggest. Can I change the project so that it will work for my child?

Although all of the activities have age guidelines attached, most of them can be adjusted to fit your child. A child is never too young to try an activity if she shows some interest. Conversely, many older children can enjoy activities intended for a younger audience, provided that you make a few minor adjustments to make it more challenging for them. Here are some guidelines to go by:

For Younger Children

- Use fewer materials: paint with just one color, color with one marker, make a collage using just paste and cotton balls
- If the materials are too large, (e.g., the mural paper is so big that your child cannot color a large portion in one sitting) make the size of the project smaller; in this case, use smaller paper.
- If the materials are too small (e.g., the beads for the necklaces are too small for your child to thread), make the size of the project bigger. For example, use larger beads for stringing.
- Assist your child with parts of the project that he cannot do himself.
- Supervise your child closely if you are working with any small pieces that could be a safety concern.

For Older Children

- Use more materials: add variety to collage materials with materials like ribbon, Mylar, colored cellophane, sandpaper, and other papers with different textures.

- Use a combination of materials to complete or expand an activity: make a painting and then attach collage materials to the wet paint. When it's dry, add Cray-Pas or marker.
- Come back to a project for more than one sitting. Start something large, like a mural or a play dough village, that you can work on over a period of time.
- Make projects to give as special gifts to family and friends.
- Combine art projects with prewriting activities. Read a favorite story and ask your child to use the materials to make one of the characters or a scene from the story.
- Give your child a problem to solve, like "Which of the items in this pile do you think will float in water? Which do you think will sink?" She can make up a hypothesis and then test it by conducting her own experiment.
- Choose activities that your child can work on with other children. Group projects build cooperation and sharing skills.
- Display your child's artwork.